THE 15 Minute MONEY MANAGER

Bob & Emilie Barnes

HARVEST HOUSE PUBLISHERS
Eugene, Oregon 97402

Portions of this book are adapted from Emilie Barnes, *The 15-Minute Organizer* (Harvest House, 1991).

THE 15-MINUTE MONEY MANAGER

Copyright © 1993 by Harvest House Publishers
Eugene, Oregon 97402

Library of Congress Cataloging-in-Publication Data
Barnes, Robert Greeley, 1930-
    The 15-minute money manager / Bob and Emilie Barnes.
      p.   cm.
    ISBN 1-56507-040-2
    1. Finance, Personal.   I. Barnes, Emilie.   II. Title.
   III. Title: Fifteen-minute money manager.
   HG179.B323   1993   92-30257
   332.024—dc20   CIP

Printed in the United States of America.

*We dedicate this book to
all the people who have influenced us
to be good stewards of
all that God has given us—
health, intelligence, talents,
marriage, relationships, and money.*

CONTENTS

Part Six:
Your Children's Money Management

Part Seven:
Good Consumer, Good Manager

   Notes

The Road to
Financial Freedom

Emilie and I were both raised in families which gave us the opportunity to work and earn money at very early ages. We learned how to be frugal with our money, how to postpone gratification, how to live within our means, and how to save for the future.

We truly appreciate the opportunity to pass on to you all that we have learned regarding the awesome subject of money. We pray that this book will have lifestyle-changing impact on you. We hope you will be inspired to learn and adopt some of these basic financial principles.

New knowledge will be effective only if you put it into action. Read this book with a highlighter pen in hand so you can mark the areas that speak to you. Don't hesitate to underline or write notes in the margin.

Make a pledge to yourself that each day you will put at least one new idea into practice.

We recognize that we are all very busy people who have difficulty finding time to read or learn new ideas. If that's you and your family, we have written this book just for you!

This 15-minute approach has short, concise chapters for reading while waiting in line, waiting for an appointment, or sitting in bed at night. After reading this book once, you will want to use it as a reference book. Put it on a shelf where it will be handy to consult again and again as you work on the family finances.

Are you in debt over your head? Is there too much month left at the end of your paycheck? Do you wonder where all your money went? Are debtors calling and asking when they can expect their money?

For the Christian family, good money management is important because God associates a person's ability to handle spiritual matters with the ability to handle money:

If you are untrustworthy about worldly wealth, who will trust you with the true riches of heaven? (Luke 16:11 TLB).

In addition, we are stewards (managers) for God of our lives and possessions, since both belong to Him. It is God who gives us power to obtain money (Deuteronomy 8:18).

Robert J. Hastings wrote, "Money management is basically self-control, for unless one learns to control himself, he is no more likely to control his money than he is to discipline his habits, his time or his temper. Undisciplined money usually spells undisciplined persons."

We learn self-control in the use of money by obtaining a proper attitude about money. Good money management is not bondage; it is freedom from the "right" to do what we want, giving us instead the *power* to do what we should!

Our goal as Christians should be to obtain financial freedom. This has four characteristics:

- ▲ Our assets exceed our liabilities.

- ▲ We are able to pay our bills as they fall due.

- ▲ We have no unpaid bills. (We are repaying per our agreement.)

- ▲ We are content with where we are.

This book will show you how to make these four elements a reality in your life. But first, there is something you must understand: *Contentment* is absolutely crucial for the other three elements to function properly. Throughout Scripture we are told to be content (1 Timothy 6:8; Hebrews 13:5; Philippians 4:12,13).

We have a saying around the Barnes household: **"If we aren't content with what we have, we will never be content with what we want."**

Money management is really more about your *attitude toward the use of money* than a systematic plan to which you become a servant. The first half of the book gives a basis for looking at money properly, and the second half offers insight into how to specifically manage your money.

May this book help you on your road toward financial freedom!

PART ONE

A Plan for Your Life

▲ ▲ ▲

$ Schedule a Plan, $
Plan a Schedule

As Emilie and I travel all over the United States and Canada, we find that a majority of individuals, couples, and families have never taken the time to develop a written statement of purpose for their lives.

If you don't know what your purpose, goals, values, and priorities are in life, you will never be able to manage your time, life, self, home, job, or money. You must schedule a plan and plan a schedule.

Charles J. Givens states, "The difference between those who accomplish their dreams and those who only dream of accomplishing them is planning and control."[1]

Many of us don't want to take the time or effort to develop sound strategies to be successful in life. There are those who want to be controlled by life rather than controlling life. These people will usually end up angry, cynical, frustrated, and disappointed with the hand that life has dealt them. On the other hand, people who seem to control life end up satisfied, joyful, and successful. They have a gleam to their radiances.

The second group of people develop a strategic plan to control their lives (with one large segment on knowing how to manage their money). A reporter once asked Helen Keller, "What would be worse than being born blind?" Miss Keller responded, "To be born with eyes, but not to have a vision."

In our Working Woman's Seminar, we give a very simple definition of success: "A Progressive Realization of Worthwhile Goals." In managing money we could paraphrase it into: "A Progressive Realization of Your Financial Objectives on a Timely and Preplanned Basis."[2]

I have a hunch that the two words "progressive realization" already concern you. We have all been conformed by our culture to believe that results must be fast or else we lose patience, become restless, and want to make things happen by our own efforts. However, this concept means a slow realization of financial objectives. Be *patient*—a hard word for Americans to understand, especially young Americans. The products of the '60s, '70s, and '80s have been led to believe "I must have it *now*—no waiting allowed." The recession of the early '90s, however, is showing some return to valuing the "progressive realization" principle of life.

Paul, the writer of Romans, shares with us a basic principle for us to consider:

> Do not be conformed to this world, but be transformed by the renewing of your mind, that you may prove what the will of God is, that which is good and acceptable and perfect (Romans 12:2).

As Christians we are at war between "conformed" and "transformed." Everywhere we turn we are pressed into being conformed to the world's mindset. Without a plan for our new lives that is the way we will go. Humans seem to take the road of least resistance. In Proverbs 29:18 we read, "Where there is no vision the people are unrestrained, but happy is he who keeps the law."

This book is meant to challenge you to live a life transformed to godly principles so that you may prove what the will of God is regarding money matters, and what is good, acceptable, and perfect in Scripture.

The next few chapters will develop the four basic components of your plan to create the spirit of "Progressive Realization of Worthwhile Goals":

▲ Developing a purpose or mission for your life.

▲ Developing goals for this purpose or mission.

▲ Planning your goals to accomplishing your purpose or mission.

▲ Scheduling these goals to accomplish your purpose or mission.

▲ Developing projects to meet your purpose or mission.

Your *purpose* or mission in life lets you state why you do what you do; your *goals* are simple statements that can be measured to help you reach your dreams with a deadline; your *planning* lets you identify a "to-do list" in implementing these goals and dreams; *scheduling* helps you put some time limits on the accomplishments—one year, three years, five years; *projects* help you visualize what projects can let you develop a master plan to accomplish your purpose or mission in life.

Let's begin by stating a purpose or mission in life.

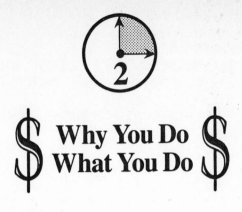

$ Why You Do $
What You Do

*No one can serve two masters. Either he will hate the
one and love the other, or he will be devoted to the one and
despise the other. You cannot serve both God and Money.*

—Matthew 6:24 NIV

My father always used to tell me, "It's not how
much money you make that counts; it's what
you do with what you make." Dad realized that there had to be a
method and a plan in managing money. It is much easier to accumulate wealth by wisely using money you save than by going out and
earning more money.

I have a very good friend who often uses the familiar saying
"Compound interest is the eighth wonder of the world." He and I
both have learned over the years the value of "progressive realization." In order to benefit from compounded interest you must have a
plan and you must be patient. (In a later chapter we will talk more
about this eighth wonder.)

In determining "Why you do what you do," you must have a basic
understanding of three basic principles of life:

▲ You must have a sense of mastery.
▲ You must have a sense of a calling.
▲ You must be willing to live life on the transformed
   plane rather than the conformed plane.

A Sense of Mastery

When we have insight into God's overall purpose for His children in this world, we have a sense of direction. In Proverbs we see that God is in control and that He truly has a master plan for our lives:

> The plans of the heart belong to man, but the answer of the tongue is from the Lord (Proverbs 16:1).
>
> The mind of man plans his way, but the Lord directs his steps (Proverbs 16:9).

Sometimes in life we take much of the credit for our success when in reality it all belongs to God. He is the Alpha and the Omega, the beginning and the end.

When we begin to realize where everything comes from, and that it is all God's and that He merely loans it to us for a short time, then we can begin to realize a humbling sense of who we are in this thing called life.

A Sense of Calling

In the big picture we must realize that we are called according to God's purpose for our lives: "We know that God causes all things to work together for good to those who love God, to those who are *called* according to His purpose" (Romans 8:28); "[He] called us with a holy *calling*, not according to our works, but according to His own purpose" (2 Timothy 1:9). A sense of calling allows us to see the big picture of God's work in our lives and helps us find meaning in our lives. Understanding our calling and purpose in life has everything to do with our identity. I hear many people today say something like "I'm going to take off six months from my job, my husband, my children, etc. to find out who I am."

When a person makes this kind of comment I realize that he or she doesn't understand that we each have a unique calling from God. By delving into the Bible we soon begin to realize that all of us have been called to serve God according to His purpose rather than ours.

One of the end results of sitting down and writing your mission or purpose in life is that you are confronted with the basic question "Why do I do what I do?" When you are able to answer this question in somewhat clear terms, then you are ready to develop strategy for your life. *This question must be answered first.*

Are you driven by expectations from outside over which you have no control, or are you inner-controlled, choosing to be what you are? When you take control of your life rather than letting life's events control you, you will see a new meaning to your life. Each day will be a new day; you will rise out of bed and vault into a new day. You will excitedly anticipate newness in your life. The Lord says, "God sees not as man sees, for man looks at the outward appearance, but the Lord looks at the heart" (1 Samuel 16:7).

The Transformed Plan
Versus the Conformed Plan

In the previous chapter we discussed this concept briefly, but we must come to grips with this contrast, because we will continually be spending wasted energy, money, and time on this wrestling match until we come to grips with this struggle.

As a young man I wanted to be able to straddle the fence and serve both masters, but as I have gotten older (and hopefully more mature and wiser) I see more clearly the giant fight for our mind. We must continually struggle for a transformed mind, or else we will fall back into a state of complacency and be conformed to the world's way of thinking. Our daily choice must be: "Whatever is true, whatever is honorable, whatever is right, whatever is pure, whatever is lovely, whatever is of good repute, if there is any excellence, and if anything worthy of praise, let your mind dwell on these things" (Philippians 4:8).

Another Barnes Motto is: **Who you will be in the next five years depends on three things:**

▲ The books you read

▲ The people you meet

▲ The choices you make

Choose today to live a transformed life!

Developing a Purpose in Life

As we look at our "triangle of success" we notice that the foundation and basic building block is the writing out of our basic purpose for life. You might think of this as being your mission in life. The first step is to create a statement which lets you begin realizing why you do what you do. From this statement you will add the other components which lead to successful financial living.

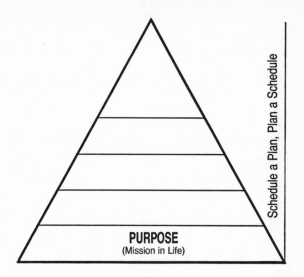

The biggest reason we don't realize what we want out of life is that we think in the negative. We see what we lack:

▲ Money
▲ Education
▲ Looks
▲ Ability
▲ Encouragement from family and friends
▲ Background

Another Barnes Motto is: **It's not what you are that holds you back, it's what you think you are not.**

The truth is that none of the above six negatives is necessary to possess in order to gain success in life. In reading biographies of past and present successful people we see that many of them started with very little. *It's what you do with what you have that counts.*

In working through this statement you need to think of your values and beliefs. If your statement isn't consistent with these two aspects of what you want out of life, you will continually have conflict in stating what you want out of life.

Values are not facts but simply choices, initially made for us by our parents and our childhood environment. As we grow and mature, our values should tend to become our own choices. The ability to choose our own values is the freedom to choose the direction for our lives.

When you act in accordance with your values you experience emotional balance, a sense of security and pleasure. When your actions are out of alignment with your values, you experience fear, guilt, frustration, and emotional imbalance. Fortunately, you can get rid of those unwanted negative feelings. You can either:

1. Change your actions to align with your values, or
2. Change your values to align with your actions.

Of course, you cannot do either until you identify what your values are.

Values are programs in the mind and can be changed only with constant prodding, attention and affirmation. In other words, to change what you value, even if change is in your best interest, you must reprogram what is in your mind. It is easier, though not usually as rewarding, to change your actions—to get rid of the conflicts and live your life in accordance with what you already value most.

Surprisingly, there are a total of only about 25 major values in life, and these values in different combinations result in the differences in people's actions. The differences in the wants, desires and objectives people set for themselves are the direct result of different values.

By identifying and prioritizing your current values, you will be able to:

▲ Set your goals to enable you to spend more of your life and money doing and experiencing those things that are most important to you.

▲ Eliminate values conflict by making certain no two values are pulling you in opposite directions.

▲ Create an environment of mutual support in your personal relationships by realizing that two people do not need the same values to create a successful relationship, but they must be able to support each other's values emotionally and financially.

▲ Determine how important wealth building is to the success of your total financial plan.

As you can see, values must be identified before goals are set or it becomes all too easy to establish one or more goals that are in conflict with your values. Reaching a goal should create a sense of accomplishment, self-confidence, excitement and a desire to celebrate, but if that goal is in conflict with an important value, there will instead be a feeling of empty achievement, frustration and sometimes even anger.[1]

Emilie and I have chosen a verse of Scripture stating our purpose in life: "Seek first His kingdom and His righteousness, and all these things shall be added to you" (Matthew 6:33). All of our life decisions are tested by this verse of Scripture. Will a particular decision pass this litmus test? If it doesn't, we don't do it.

Our theologian forefathers expressed the chief end of man this way: "The chief end of man is to glorify God and to enjoy Him forever." This too would make a great statement of purpose.

Henrietta Mears once stated, "There is no magic in small plans. When I consider my ministry, I think of the world. Anything less than that would not be worthy of Christ nor His will for my life."

Bill Bright, founder and President of Campus Crusade for Christ, selected in the early part of 1950 his verse to define his purpose for life. It is known as the Great Commission:

> Go therefore and make disciples of all the nations, baptizing them in the name of the Father and the Son and the Holy Spirit, teaching them to observe all that I commanded you; and lo, I am with you always, even to the end of the age (Matthew 28:19,20).

Over the past 40 years, Campus Crusade has been led by the statement of this purpose in life. Those who know Bill Bright and Campus Crusade's ministry can testify of their adherence to this statement.

You may want to write out what you want to accomplish in life as a statement that will be your guiding force for establishing goals for your plan.

Remember that a statement is general in nature and is not meant to be stated in strictly measurable terms.

The Barnes' Purpose of Life is stated as: *"Seek first His Kingdom and His righteousness, and all these things shall be added to you."*

In the space provided below, write out your statement of purpose.

My purpose of life is: _____

_____

_____

Hang on to this statement, because everything else we do in this section will be based upon this statement.

You may change your statement of purpose at any time. It is not set in concrete, but is merely a base for all the other decisions in planning for a meaningful life.

$ Goals: A Dream $
with a Deadline

What you commit yourself to become determines what you are.

—Tony Campolo

Goals prod us into action. They are a means to an end. A well-stated goal has three qualities:

▲ It states *quantity* (be specific).
▲ It gives a *deadline* (starting and completion dates).
▲ It is *written out* (though not in concrete).

"I want to lose 15 pounds by July 1." That is very brief but it meets the two basic criteria of a goal. Goals are measurable, whereas purposes aren't that specific. I like to tell those who attend our seminars that goals are dreams with a deadline.

These stated goals are specific objectives on which you have decided to invest your time, money, and energy. A goal can be accomplished very quickly or it may take a lifetime. Only state those goals which are in keeping with your value system and which help you meet your stated purpose of life.

Each year between Christmas and the first part of January we take a vacation trip to some place where we can kick back, relax, recreate, and plan for the new year. We each spend the first couple of days writing out two or three goals under the following topics:

▲ **Spiritual goals**	Activities to strengthen your spiritual life together
▲ **Physical goals**	Things you want to do physically
▲ **Family goals**	Activities you want to do to bring closer relationships
▲ **Financial goals**	What you want to do with your finances
▲ **Professional goals**	Courses to be taken, seminars to attend, books to read
▲ **Mental goals**	Projects for the brain
▲ **Social goals**	Activities to do which would include your friends, old and new
▲ **Community support goals**	Involvements to support the community.

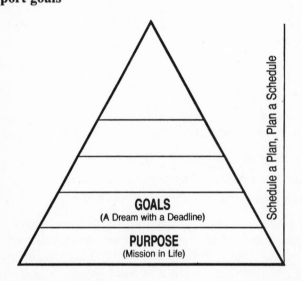

Emilie does her set of goals and I do mine. On the third or fourth day we come together and discuss each of our goals for the new year. After some time discussing together, we write out the "Barnes Goals" for the new year.

Be committed. Your level of commitment to any goal determines how you will handle interferences along the way. Remember that these goals aren't set in concrete; they can be changed or altered.

Don't just think or dream about your various goals. Put them in writing on paper or enter them into your computer. Somehow the physical activity of writing them out gives greater credibility to their value. Make lists similar to the ones shown in this chapter, but don't just write them and file them away. Keep them where you can refer to them from time to time. Emilie and I keep them in the front of our Bibles, and we review them at least once a quarter. Sometimes we change an entry, and sometimes we confirm that we are on target and move on.

Emilie's book *Survival for Busy Women* provides two charts which are used to track personal goals! One chart is designed for the person who has never kept goals before. It is bite-sized, with no more than three months of goals at a time. Don't overwhelm yourself with too much to do. If you do, you will become discouraged and give up.

Remember that it takes 21 days to create a new habit.

The other chart is more sophisticated and has several new components added. There is room to state what you need to consider for each goal. You may have a wonderful goal stated, but you must take time to consider other people, costs, added education, time away from home, etc. There is also space to rank the goal by priority.

Not all goals are possible for today. Some are "A" priority (which is urgent—top of the list); some are "B" priority (which I call my "maybe items"); some are "C" priority (which I classify as no time, money, or energy given to this today). My B and C items can become A's, but not for now.

Another necessary section for your goal list is space to jot down your steps to completing this specific goal. Think through the various steps necessary, and then jot these down in this area. You also have a space to date the beginning and another space to jot the completion.

ONE WOMAN'S
THREE-MONTH GOALS

Objectives	Jan. - Feb.- March Activity Period		Target Date	Goals Realized
Personal				
1. Read: Loving God by Colson			2/1	1/18
2. Lose 5 pounds			3/1	3/6
Family				
1. Have a short devotion at breakfast			1/1	
2. Be a blessing to each other			1/1	
Career				
1. Enroll in "Elementary Accounting" at Local College			1/6	1/6
2. Apply for new position opening at work			1/15	1/15
Church				
1. Volunteer to be an usher			1/9	1/10

GOALS

TIME PERIOD	DATE

GOAL: *I will revise my will by March 1st*   **PRIORITY:** *A*

CONSIDER: *New life insurance-dependents*

No.	STEPS	DATE	✔
1	Call for Appointment	1/2	✓
2	Appointment at 10:00 for 2/3		

GOAL: *I will lose 5 lbs. by February 15*   **PRIORITY:** *A*

CONSIDER: *Have a physical/checkup by doctor*

No.	STEPS	DATE	✔
1.	Join an Aerobics Class	1/3	✓
2.	Begin Jan 6th	1/3	
3.	Modify my eating habits	1/4	
	A. Eliminate sugar		
4.	Physical exam – Jan. 9th 9:00	1/4	

GOAL: *I will join a Women's Bible Study*   **PRIORITY:** __

CONSIDER: *Children's School Schedule*

No.	STEPS	DATE	✔
1.	Call Church office for schedule	1/4	✓
2.	Class begins January 14th at 10 A.M.	1/4	

$ Writing Your Financial Goals $

E ach of us has similar financial goals, but varying somewhat based upon our personal value system. These goals would include:

1. Income goals—the increases in yearly income we want to achieve.

2. Career goals—the type of work we want to do, the company positions we want to attain, or the business we want to create.

3. Acquisition goals—the things we want to buy and own.

4. Travel goals—the places nationally and internationally we want to visit and experience.

5. Accomplishment goals—the things we want to do and become.

6. Educational goals—the knowledge we want to acquire for personal, financial, and career advancement.

7. Recreational vehicle goals—the "fun" things we want to own for recreation and sports.

8. Investment goals—the income-producing, tax-reducing, or net-worth-increasing investments we want to own.

Income Goals

In order to accomplish these financial goals we have to take a serious look at our income goals. And we need to be realistic in this area. Many couples get into real trouble by being too optimistic when deciding if their present income is going to let them establish attainable goals for their immediate future. If you are single, either male or female, you have little chance of increasing your income substantially unless you get a sizable raise, inherit money, or marry.

When Emilie and I were first married, she worked in a bank for the first three years. It would have been very easy to increase our standard of living with the extra money, but we didn't. We tucked most of it away into a savings account for a down payment on that first home.

Over the last few years about 4 to 5 percent of yearly income has been used to keep up with inflation. If your income doesn't grow by at least this amount you are losing ground to inflation.

A basic question is, "Will your current rate of increase allow you to finance your dreams?" That depends upon two things: 1) the amount of time it will take you to double your income after inflation is factored in, and 2) how much of a hurry you are in to reach your dreams. (Remember, success is a progressive realization of worthwhile goals.)

Ways to Increase Your Income If You Work for Someone Else[1]

- ▲ Increase your skill level, education, or profile in your present job.
- ▲ Create a new, better-paying job in your department and fill it.
- ▲ Seek promotion to another department.
- ▲ Ask for raises as you go the extra mile.
- ▲ Change companies for greater opportunities.
- ▲ Change to a higher-paying career by getting the necessary skills or education.

Ways to Increase Your Income If You Work for Yourself

- ▲ Increase sales through hiring more salespeople or spending a greater portion of your time selling.

▲ Create a better advertising and marketing campaign.

▲ Cut your expenses in every area without sacrificing net profit.

▲ Expand your line of products or services.

Career Goals

Here are guidelines that will help you determine the directions in which you would like to take your career.

1. Do you want to change careers?   Yes ___   No ___
   To what kind of work?

   1. _____   3. _____

   2. _____   4. _____

2. Do you want your own business?   Yes ___   No ___
   In what kind of work?

   1. _____   3. _____

   2. _____   4. _____

3. Advances you want to make in your present career:

	Position	**Annual Salary**
Current	_____	$ _____
1 year	_____	$ _____
5 years	_____	$ _____

Acquisition Goals

Make a list of all the things you would like to own, how much they cost, and the date by which you hope to acquire them. Include automobiles, stereos, jewelry, furs, furniture, clothes, etc. Some items will come from your "dreams list."

	Item	**Cost (Approx.)**	**Target Date (Mo./Yr.)**
1.	_____	_____	_____
2.	_____	_____	_____
3.	_____	_____	_____

4. _____ _____ _____
5. _____ _____ _____
6. _____ _____ _____
7. _____ _____ _____
8. _____ _____ _____
9. _____ _____ _____
10. _____ _____ _____

Travel Goals

Make a list of the top ten places which you would like to visit in the United States and abroad. Your list can include the names of countries, states, cities, monuments, or other attractions.

	Destination	**Target Date (Mo./Yr.)**
1.	_____	_____
2.	_____	_____
3.	_____	_____
4.	_____	_____
5.	_____	_____
6.	_____	_____
7.	_____	_____
8.	_____	_____
9.	_____	_____
10.	_____	_____

Accomplishment Goals

Make a list of all the things you want to do and become. Include positions you would like to hold in clubs, groups, your church, and your community. Include sports in which you would like to get involved or to excel, as well as social activities or organizations you want to join. Also, list the awards you want to win or other forms of recognition you want to achieve.

	Sport, Activity, or Organization	What You Want to Accomplish	Target Date (Mo./Yr.)
1.	_____	_____	_____
2.	_____	_____	_____
3.	_____	_____	_____
4.	_____	_____	_____
5.	_____	_____	_____

Educational Goals

Make a list of the courses or programs you would like to take and the estimated cost of each. Examples: Speed-reading courses, night-school course, courses to complete your degree, real estate investing programs.

	Program	Approximate Starting Date	Approximate Cost
1.	_____	_____	$ _____
2.	_____	_____	$ _____
3.	_____	_____	$ _____
4.	_____	_____	$ _____
5.	_____	_____	$ _____

Recreational Vehicle Goals

Make a list of the recreational vehicles you would like to own, when you want to acquire them, and the cost of each.

		Type	Acquire	Cost
1.	Sports car	_____	_____	_____
2.	Motorcycle	_____	_____	_____
3.	Bicycle	_____	_____	_____
4.	Snowmobile	_____	_____	_____
5.	Sailboat	_____	_____	_____

6. Jet Ski/ _____ _____ _____
   wet bike
7. Fishing boat _____ _____ _____

8. Hobie Cat _____ _____ _____

9. Sailboard _____ _____ _____

10. Houseboat _____ _____ _____

11. Yacht _____ _____ _____

12. Airplane _____ _____ _____

13. Hang glider _____ _____ _____

14. Motor home _____ _____ _____

15. Camper _____ _____ _____

Investment Goals

There is only one reason to invest: to accumulate money to buy yourself something in the future that you can't afford now. For some people this means financially safe and secure retirement years. Other people have goals that won't wait until retirement, and investing means eventually having the money to make the down payment on a beautiful home or expensive automobile, or having a cushion to quit a job and start a business. Investment accounts, retirement accounts, and investment in your home and other real estate are all means you can use to achieve your investment goals. Your goals list will help you determine how important your investment plan will become to your future.

Make an Investment Goals Chart similar to the one below to identify where you are now and where you want to be the next year, five years from now, and at age 65. This chart will also help you measure your progress.

INVESTMENT GOALS CHART

	This Year	Next Year	5 Years	Age 65
Cash in bank	$ _____	$ _____	$ _____	$ _____
Investment accounts	$ _____	$ _____	$ _____	$ _____

Retirement accounts	$ ____	$ ____	$ ____	$ ____
Your home	$ ____	$ ____	$ ____	$ ____
Real estate investments	$ ____	$ ____	$ ____	$ ____
Other investments	$ ____	$ ____	$ ____	$ ____
TOTAL	$ ____	$ ____	$ ____	$ ____

Here are some suggestions that will help you fill in your Investment Goals Chart:

Cash in bank. Include for this year all money in bank-type savings and checking accounts, money market accounts, or any other cash. Set your goals for the future on the level of available cash that will give you a sense of security.

Investment accounts. Include all stocks, bonds, CD's, government securities, and mutual fund shares you now own, plus what you want to have invested in the future.

Retirement accounts. Enter the amount of money currently in all your retirement accounts. Your retirement accounts will cover the cost of your lifestyle after you are no longer producing income from your job or career. By the time you retire, the amount in your retirement plan should be eight times the annual income you want to have during your retirement years. Although other investments may also produce income during your retirement years, here you will list only the amounts you have and want to have in your retirement accounts, including your IRA, SEP, Keogh, 401(k), 403(b), annuities, federal retirement plan, state retirement plan, and union retirement plan.

Your home. Show the current amount of unmortgaged equity you have in your home—what your home is worth minus what you owe. For future years, estimate what you think your home should be worth. If your goal is to buy a more expensive home, adjust your estimated home equity accordingly. If you own or plan to own a second home, show those figures also.

Real estate investments. Show the equity you have in rental real estate or land and the equity you would like to have in the future.

Other assets. Include the value of such noninvestment assets as automobiles, jewelry, furniture, etc.

I can't overemphasize the importance of putting all your financial goals in writing. Focusing on your goals inevitably means that you will think about how to achieve them. Putting them in writing motivates you to take the necessary actions.

$ Making Your $ "To Do" List

Which one of you, when he wants to build a tower, does not first sit down and calculate the cost, to see if he has enough to complete it? Otherwise, when he has laid a foundation, and is not able to finish, all who observe it begin to ridicule him, saying, "This man began to build and was not able to finish."

—Luke 14:28-30

Planning is crucial if we are going to realize our purpose in life. Christ pointed out to His disciples the high cost of commitment to His calling, and we are likewise to realize that planning makes similar demands of our lives.

I am continually told by the women who come to our seminars that their husbands aren't interested in this whole process of planning for the future. Men must wake up and get serious with life.

Procrastination

Many people are paralyzed because of their inability to make a decision and get their gearshift into drive. One of the ways we are ineffective in our lives is by the evil time-waster called *procrastination*.

In adults, procrastination generally signals some kind of internal conflict. After we have made the decision to do something, a part of us still holds us back. Why do we hold back?

▲ We feel overwhelmed.

▲ We overestimate the amount of time needed.

▲ We would rather be doing something else.

▲ We think that if we wait long enough, the task will go away.

▲ We fear failure.

▲ We fear success.

▲ We enjoy the last-minute adrenaline rush.

Ways to Stop Procrastinating

▲ Make yourself a "to do" list. Use the last five to seven minutes of each day to jot down several activities that need to be done tomorrow (see sample list at the end of this chapter).

▲ Keep a log of how long various projects take (usually shorter than you thought).

▲ Work with the time available to you, breaking the task into small bites. Call these "instant tasks." You get a lot of satisfaction in completing these small tasks. See Emilie's book *The 15-Minute Organizer* for more ideas on this concept.

▲ Make time by saying no to lesser projects and blocks of time.

▲ Set small deadlines for these small tasks.

▲ Do things as they come to you.

▲ Ask yourself, "Is there a simpler way?"

▲ Eliminate distractions.

▲ Make it easy to work by grouping like things together. Make them handy.

▲ Reward yourself for getting started.

▲ Tell someone else what your deadline is.

▲ Expect problems; things don't always go as expected.

▲ Learn to delegate.

▲ Start today; don't wait for tomorrow!

DAILY REMINDER

DATE: 5-14

Call:

1. Ben's Plumbing
   555-4221

2. Insurance-Car
   555-4702

3. Lamb School
   Jenny's Teacher
   555-9990

4.

5. Pastor Cook
   555-0233

Do:

1. Take clothes
   to Cleaners

2. Car Pool driver
   this week

3. Take dinner
   to Merrihaus

4. Visit Mrs. Jones
   at Hospital

5.

See:

1. That Chad gets
   homework done

2. Hubby for
   lunch

3. Barbara D.
   at ballgame

4. That Christine's
   dress is hemmed

5. Focus on the family
   on T.V. @ 8:00 P.M.

$ Scheduling Goals for Peak Performance $

There is an appointed time for everything, and there is a time for every event under heaven.

—Ecclesiastes 3:1

If we have a proper overview of life, we realize that there is an appointed time for every event of our lives. Truly there is a God who masterminds all of life's events, there is a calling which we all have, and there is a world of contrast living (conforming versus transforming).

As I look back over life, I realize that there are definite seasons of life. What you do at 50 isn't available to you at 30, and what was available at 30 isn't available to you at 50. The mystery that amazes me is that God's timing is always perfect; there are no flaws or mistakes.

Since people tend to be "now"-oriented, the general public has a very difficult time waiting on the Lord.

When our children were very young, our family attended a summer camp at Forest Home Christian Conference Center in Southern California. One of the speakers addressed the idea that we needed to plan and think what we wanted our children to be as teenagers. At that time Jenny was about seven and Brad was about five years old, and I thought, *No problem, I won't have to think about that for several years.* Wrong! He said, "Start scheduling now." I said, "But Jenny won't be a teenager for another six years!" "Schedule now for the future, it will soon be here," he said.

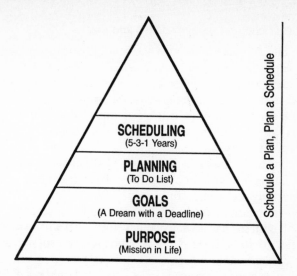

Many couples say, "I don't know what we are going to do next week, let alone three to five years from now."

I'm so glad that Emilie and I made a commitment during that week to schedule for the future. Once we started thinking several years ahead of time we could think of projects to get us successfully to that point in time.

When we sold our manufacturing company several years ago, I sold my stock and cashed in my profit-sharing funds and was left with no retirement plans for the future. One of my financial goals that year was to set up an Individual Retirement Account (IRA) and a self-directed profit-sharing account (Keogh) to help with Social Security funds for our retirement.

That goal made me future-oriented; I had to get beyond the present and think several years into the future. It takes proper scheduling to be on target for the retirement season of your life. You need to schedule:

▲ Where you will be in five years
▲ Your children's education
▲ The status of your marriage
▲ Your career level
▲ Where you will live

▲ Your retirement

▲ Your children's future mates and their weddings

For about 25 years Emilie and I had been praying for our children's future mates. We knew they were born and living and being raised somewhere. We prayed for God's protection, and for their moral and character development as youngsters. *We* wanted them to be godly and possess a teachable spirit. Do you know what? That's exactly what God gave us in Craig Merrihew for our daughter and Maria McCallum for our son.

The most marvelous scheduling was God's creating me in time. He planned me from the very beginning. The writer of Psalms says, "I am fearfully and wonderfully made" (see Psalm 139:13,14).

There are many financial goals that need to be scheduled *now*. Don't wait until the day actually comes, for then it will be too late to control the situation. Instead, the situation will control *you*, and you will not be the winner.

So activate now! What needs to be scheduled right now? Write it down or it will float away.

1. *Schedule an appointment with my attorney for a will.*

2. *Open an IRA at my bank.*

3. _____

4. _____

5. _____

6. _____

7. _____

Our goals can be designed to be scheduled in three categories: short-term goals, mid-term goals, and long-term goals. Anything less than a month is considered short-term; two months to two years would be mid-term goals; two to five years would be long-term goals.

Lifetime Goals	short-term goals	mid-term goals	long-term goals	**Lifetime Goals**

Notice that at the front of the diagram is Lifetime Goals and at the tail of the diagram is Lifetime Goals. They are at the beginning of the process as well as the end of the process. As we decided to plan for our children to be free, strong, and committed young people living out their own unique gifts, we had to schedule projects that were short-term (daily) as well as long-term. If not, it would never happen later.

Many authorities on this subject believe that you need to visualize a goal already fulfilled and to store that picture in your mind as one of the most successful ways to reach a goal.

The Wright brothers had a dream to become the first men to fly. Everyone thought they were crazy, but on December 17, 1903, they achieved their personal dream goal.

Write down several goals that would be under each category.

Short-term goals (less than one month)
  A. To open a money market savings account by the end of the month.
  B.
  C.
  D.
  E.

Mid-term goals (two months to two years)
  A. Register for an accounting class by December 15.
  B.
  C.
  D.
  E.

Long-term goals (two to five years)
  A. Purchase a retirement home within 36 months.
  B.
  C.
  D.
  E.

Projects Designed for Success

The greatest thing in the world is not so much where we start as in what direction we're moving.

—Oliver Wendell Holmes

I hope the last few chapters have captured your vision for planning, not only for your life in general but also for the various aspects which make up your life. The rest of this book will deal specifically with projects you can do to increase your financial independence.

Projects are activities which assist us to reach our purpose in life. They will be different for each of us. The project is what puts our focused energy into action. The following listing will give you an idea how it may work.

Area: *Financial*

Goal: *To be able to build our dream home and to finance our three-week vacation*

Ten-Year Goal Activities

1. To move into our 2500-square-foot, three-bedroom home on one acre of land with a mortgage of $90,000 and with no more than a $1200 monthly payment.

2. To enjoy a three-week vacation with the family with no more than $500 being financed for this trip.

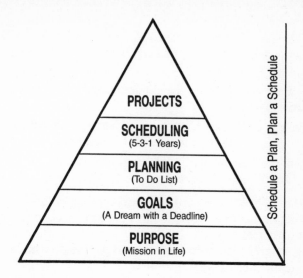

Five-Year Goal Activities

1. To purchase our one-acre parcel and begin a five-year payment plan.
2. To plan a two-week vacation in the mountains. Emphasis on the finance and budget for this vacation.

Three-Year Goal Activities

1. To research and investigate the various aspects in purchasing, financing, and designing our new home.
2. To plan a one-week vacation trip to the beach; emphasis on hope to finance the trip.

One-Year Goal Activities

1. To meet with the bank to determine a savings plan that will let us meet our financial goal of building our own home and taking a three-week vacation.
2. To begin a savings plan to meet the two ten-year goals.

Today's Goal Activities

1. To make an appointment to meet with the loan officer of our main branch bank.

2. To visit the main library and talk to the librarian about her recommendation of the two best architect magazines for our style of living.

3. To sit down and talk with the children about how they can help with this plan.

4. To purchase a qualified camping/vacation magazine that describes various planning aspects for successful vacations.

5. To go to the Automobile Club to acquire various maps showing details for our minivacations.

If we are to live life on purpose, our composite of lifetime goals helps us determine what we do today. This way we control life and don't let it control us.

Another Barnes Motto is: **"Successful people do what unsuccessful people aren't willing to do."**

It takes choices for us to live this way. It isn't easy, but the difference is certainly worth the effort. Each day when I wake up I have to choose to make meaningful decisions today. Each of us has 24 hours or 1440 minutes or 86,400 seconds in each day. Those who get the most out of life are those who make wise decisions based upon what life means to them. Live life with a purpose!

People don't plan to fail, but they do plan to succeed. Success doesn't come by luck or accident; it comes because individuals schedule a plan and also plan a schedule.

When it comes to money matters, you must have a plan or you won't be able to make good daily decisions. Today's decisions must be based on your future orientation. No plans for the future muddy the water in deciding what to do today.

$ Putting Family Life $
Goals in Writing

I can do all things through Him who strengthens me.
—Philippians 4:13

Throughout the first seven chapters I have referred to writing down the Barnes Life Goals each year. Emilie does hers, I do mine, and then we compile a joint list for each calendar year. It is not overly sophisticated, but it works for us. You may want to design your own form. The important thing is to get started.

THE FAMILY LIFE GOALS

Theme Verse: "_____
_____**"**

My purpose or mission in life is: _____
_____

1. Spiritual   a. To read the book of John _____
   Goal
                 b. _____

When?

                 a. By May 1 _____

                 b. _____

2. Physical goal   a. To weigh   pounds _____

                         b. _____

                         When?

                         a. By July 1 _____

                         b. _____

3. Family goal   a. _____

                         b. _____

                         When?

                         a. _____

                         b. _____

4. Financial goal   a. _____

                         b. _____

                         When?

                         a. _____

                         b. _____

5. Professional goal   a. _____

                         b. _____

                         When?

                         a. _____

                         b. _____

6. Mental goal   a. _____

                         b. _____

                         When?

                         a. _____

                         b. _____

7. Social goal   a. _____

                         b. _____

                         When?

                         a. _____

                         b. _____

8. Community
   support goal

a. _____

b. _____

When?

a. _____

b. _____

The most important foundation of this form is stating your purpose or mission in life. From this statement comes the value for all other planning. Make sure your goals are consistent with your statement. If not, drop the goal or change your statement. Statement and goals must be consistent with each other.

PART TWO

The
Right Priorities

▲ ▲ ▲

$ Four Cornerstones for Money Management $

You may say to yourself, "My power and the strength of my hands have produced this wealth for me." But remember the Lord your God, for it is he who gives you the ability to produce wealth.

—Deuteronomy 8:17,18 NIV

A very good friend of ours, Jim De Lorenzo, is a bricklayer par excellence. All of the most discriminating homeowners in Riverside smile with pride when Jim can do their masonry work. He is so good that recently the California Brick Association selected him the outstanding builder for using brick as a building material. Jim has done brickwork for us in each of our homes over the last 20 years. He is the best in his profession.

The first thing he does when he gets on the job is to get out his transit and shoot the grade to make sure he knows where the cornerstone is going to be. From there everything will be built from the central calculation. All heights of retaining walls will come from there.

Several years ago we had a new garage built, and the contractor did the same measuring and calculating to determine the four cornerstones and to make sure they are level.

That's the way it is with finances: There are four basic principles that are cornerstones. In order to have a good sense and proper attitude toward money, these principles must be your basic reference for all your money decisions.

Cornerstone 1:
Recognize that God Owns Everything

He owns our home, our car, our marriage, our children, our job, our business, and our talents. We may possess them, but we don't own them. Possession is not ownership.

▲ The earth is the Lord's and all it contains, the world, and those who dwell in it (Psalm 24:1).

▲ Every beast of the forest is Mine, the cattle on a thousand hills. I know every bird of the mountains, and everything that moves in the field is Mine (Psalm 50:10,11).

▲ "The silver is Mine and the gold is Mine," declares the Lord of hosts (Haggai 2:8).

Everything belongs to God. You are merely a steward of His property. God holds you personally responsible to faithfully manage for Him whatever money or possessions He allows you to have.

Often we are tempted to grasp our possessions selfishly, as if they actually belonged to us and not to God. I'll never forget the beautiful blue 1972 Mercedes Benz I cherished for about ten years. I waxed it often to keep it shining brightly, kept it in the garage when I wasn't driving it, and dusted it every day.

Once when Emilie and I were away for a few days, our son Brad and a few buddies came home from college to go skiing. Brad saw my Mercedes in the garage and decided to take it to the mountains to impress his friends and any young ladies they might meet. He strapped the ski rack to the roof, loaded the skis and poles onto the rack, and headed for the slopes.

All went well until they started home. The ski rack vibrated loose and slid off, leaving a dent and a large scratch on the roof of my Mercedes. When I returned home, Brad broke the news. When I saw the damaged car I was angry at Brad for taking my car without asking, and devastated that he had allowed my prized car to be damaged. But it took me only a moment to regain my composure. God was using the incident to test my perspective on my car. "Well,

God, Your car has a scratch and a dent," I said. I drove God's Mercedes for another year-and-a-half with the scratched and dented roof. Each time I looked at the damage it reminded me who really owned the car.

As caretakers of God's money and property we must obediently grow and nurture the spiritual fruit of self-control. (See Galatians 5:22,23.)

Take a few minutes and jot down your possessions that God owns.

1. _____   4. _____

2. _____   5. _____

3. _____   6. _____

If you have never given them to God before, you might want to do that now. Turn everything over to him.

Cornerstone 2:
The Goal of Financial Responsibility Is Financial Freedom

In order to be financially free you must meet these qualifications:

▲ Your income exceeds your expenses.

▲ You are able to pay your debts as they fall due.

▲ You have no unpaid bills.

▲ Above all, you are content at your present income level.

We mentioned this Barnes Motto earlier: *"If you are not satisfied with what you have, you will never be satisfied with what you want."*

List three things you intend to do to become more financially free.

1. _____

2. _____

3. _____

Cornerstone 3:
Establish a Spiritual Purpose for Your Life

If your spiritual purpose is to serve God (Matthew 6:33), all of your resources become ministering currency toward that end. An example would be Patrick Morley in his book *The Man in the Mirror*. He shares a situation out of his own family's experience:

> Several years ago we began to earn more money than needed to live in the manner to which we were accustomed. We live in a neighborhood where our children are happy, secure, and settled. My wife likes the convenient location and the neighbors. One of my daughter's very best friends lives two doors down. No dogs bark in the middle of the night, and no expressway drowns out the conversation when we cook out in the backyard.

> Since we were making enough money to live in a bigger, more expensive house, I began to make plans to move. That's what people do when they can afford to, isn't it? We can generally slot people's income level by the house they live in, because most people keep trading up to the most expensive one their income will allow. People with a $25,000 income live in homes which $25,000 of income can afford; people with a $50,000 income live in homes which $50,000 of income can afford; people with a $150,000 income live in homes which $150,000 of income can afford.

> Yet we loved our neighborhood. And we know that people and relationships were more important than possessions. But the social pressure to buy the bigger house preoccupied my mind. The image of having money, and making sure everyone else knows it, pulls like a tug-of-war against the Christian life view.

> One day I noticed I was the only family member pressing for the move. That got me thinking. Finally I yielded my ambition to move to the bigger house and allowed God to work. We decided to redecorate instead.

> Over the years we began to give shape and form to the belief that God wanted us to put a cap on our standard of living. And however He blessed us over and above that standard of living, He wanted us to help fulfill His purposes.

> This decision evolved. We didn't actually sit down and write it out on a piece of paper. Rather, over time, by our lifestyles and actions, we inbred it into values. Then one day we said it out loud, and that settled the issue.

So now we live a predetermined standard of living. And everything God entrusts to us above what we need to live and save for retirement, we give to His work. I would have guessed that living in a bigger house would have made me feel more significant. Yet the sense of usefulness and the impact that we are having leaves us with a deep confidence that we are truly significant, not for our own self-gratification, but in a way that will last forever.[1]

The more money we give to God's work the more our hearts will be fixed on Him. The opposite is also true: Don't give money to God's work, and your heart will not be fixed on Him.

Write down at least one area of your life where you could change priorities and direct the monies to God's work.

1. _____

_____

Cornerstone 4:
Give Money to the Lord
on a Regular Basis

Once I heard a comic on TV say, "I've been rich and I've been poor; and I like being rich better." For the Christian, the only reason to be rich is to have resources to carry on God's program. Does God need our wealth? No. Can God's purposes be carried out without our money? Yes! God doesn't need our possessions, but we do need to give.

God doesn't care how much we give as deeply as He cares *why* we give. When we lovingly and obediently fulfill our role as givers—no matter what the amount—God will use what we give to minister to others and we will receive a blessing in return.

The Scriptures clearly show us many directions for our giving:

- ▲ To God through our tithes, gifts, and offerings (Proverbs 3:9,10; 1 Corinthians 16:2)
- ▲ To the poor (Proverbs 19:17)
- ▲ To other believers in need (Romans 12:13; Galatians 6:9,10)
- ▲ To those who minister to us (Galatians 6:6, 1 Timothy 5:17,18)

▲ To widows (1 Timothy 5:3-16)

▲ To family members (1 Timothy 5:8)

On the subject of giving to God, we have already determined that everything we have is His anyway. The question of how much we should actually give back to God in tithes, gifts, and offerings is debatable among Christians. Some insist on a literal tithe (10 percent) and others claim that grace allows each individual to give as he chooses. Without entering the debate, my point is simply that Christians are clearly instructed to return to the Owner of everything a portion of what He has given to us. I will use 10 percent to represent Christian giving, whether offered as a tithe or a freewill gift.

Second Corinthians 9:6-15 contains three excellent principles on the topic of giving. Read the passage for yourself and note the following principles:

Principle 1: We reap what we sow. If we sow sparingly we will reap sparingly. Plants cannot grow if no seeds have been planted. Cups cannot overflow unless water is continually poured into them. If you want an abundance, you must give an abundance. If you give little, you will reap little.

Principle 2: We are to be cheerful givers. We are not to give because we feel pressured to give, but freely and joyfully as in all other areas of ministry. We have attended a couple of churches which have helped worshipers grasp this truth. In the Mariner's Church in Newport Beach, California, no offering plates are passed. The church leaders believe that if God is working in your life, you will make the effort to place your gift in the mail slot in the wall. Another church we attended called the offering box in the foyer the "blessing box." Leaders in this church taught the principles of giving, then trusted parishioners to respond to God's Word instead of an offering plate. And whenever a special financial need arose, the elders brought it to the congregation and the need was met.

Principle 3: We will be blessed because of our obedience. The world will know we are obedient to God by our faithfulness in giving.

You may ask, "How can I give before I receive? Don't I need to have something before I can give it?" That may be the way we think, but that's not the way God thinks. Luke 6:38 states, "Give, and it will be given to you" (NIV). Only after we give are we ready to receive what God has for us.

Many people ask the question, "What is the right way to give money to the Lord?" I was raised with the concept of the 10 percent tithe, and that has been our guideline for returning a portion of our monies to God's work, both in the local church and to parachurch organizations. This money needs to be set aside as it is earned and then given in a systematic way each Sunday. (Even when away from the church on a Sunday we need to continue to give on a regular basis.)

There are many Christian businessmen and women who give tithes of their companies' earnings to Christian organizations. We have a builder in our city who builds a new church each year as his way of returning profits back to the Lord.

These monies are to be used in the work of the local church, but God may direct you to help other worthwhile groups that aren't church-affiliated.

In general your giving should be done in private to guard against you becoming proud or trying to control an agenda on where it should go. Remember, we are giving to God and not to man, and so we should not look for a blessing from specific churches or people to whom we give.

In order to be effective with your money, so that at the end of the month you don't ask the famous question "Where did all my money go?" you need to:

▲ Recognize that God owns everything

▲ Strive for financial freedom

▲ Establish a spiritual purpose for your life

▲ Give to the Lord's work regularly

Four Little-Known Secrets for Developing Financial Strength

A faithful man will abound with blessings.
—Proverbs 28:20

What a mystery money is! Many people spend their whole life working for it, and some even die for it, but many aren't happy with it when they get it. Money is like a gun: In the right hands it can be a tool for justice, but in the hands of a criminal it can become a weapon of evil.

Money is simply a commodity for exchange. It enables us to provide an end to a means—the purchase of something.

There are four ways in which we can get money:

▲ We can work for it.

▲ We can loan it to someone else and earn interest on it.

▲ We can subcontract it out to someone else and earn a profit from their labor.

▲ We can invest it (risk it) in order to speculate that we may earn a profit.

There are many experts in the field of Christian money management, most of whom give different formulas and principles on how to use God's resources of money. We have adopted four basic guidelines or secrets to assist us in handling money and developing a sound money-managing strategy.

Secret 1:
Earn Little by Little

The writer of Proverbs understood this concept very well, for he wrote, "Wealth obtained by fraud dwindles, but the one who gathers by labor increases it" (Proverbs 13:11). (The NIV reads, "He who gathers money little by little makes it grow.") That's the basic concept behind accumulation of excess money beyond the monthly expenses. In the first section of this book we talked about **Progressive realization of worthwhile goals**. The Lord rewards those who are patient and content with their lives. It is amazing how the consistent plodder advances in life. The prize doesn't always go to the swift. Develop a life of being satisfied with a little at a time.

Secret 2:
Save Little by Little

As a young boy delivering early morning papers and only making about $35 per month, I can remember learning this basic principle of saving some money each month. Over the years I can't remember a month when I haven't saved something. In America we are a spending country, but we must turn to becoming a saving country if we are to survive financially. One of the greatest services you can give your children is to teach them how to save on a regular basis. It teaches them to be future-oriented, and they also learn to postpone gratification.

In our country, saving for retirement seems to be on everyone's mind. Even young couples think about this great benchmark in life. We need to start early in life to save for that event.

Patrick Morley has a good chart in his book dealing with "The Nest Egg Principle."

> You can pick the annual retirement income you want. That's right. Pick any income level you want, and then follow this simple plan: Each year of your forty-year career save 10 percent of your desired annual retirement income, put it into a qualified retirement plan, and you can extend your targeted income in perpetuity.

How does that work? Here's an example:

▲ Desired annual income at retirement	$40,000
▲ Amount to save each year	$4,000
▲ Required average annual earnings rate	6.2%
▲ Number of years	40

Here are the results at retirement, rounded to the nearest thousand dollars:

▲ The nest egg (capital accumulated)	$651,000
▲ Yield required to produce desired income	6.2%
▲ Annual retirement income	$40,000

(Note: Tax and inflation consequences are not considered. Money saved can be sheltered through proper tax planning, and retirement income can be protected through lower tax rates and tax-exempt income instruments, e.g., municipal bonds.)

If you have a late start you can catch up by saving more, earning a higher interest rate, or some of each. Here are the required interest rates you would have to earn for shorter periods of time to produce the same income:

	30 years	20 years	10 years
Yield needed	8.3%	12.8%	27.0%
Capital accumulated	$479,000	$316,000	$147,000[1]

Any desired income level can be extended by saving ten percent of that amount for forty years at 6.2 percent.

Here are several ways to achieve this goal:

▲ Open an IRA account with your bank or any reputable investment broker.

▲ Contribute to your retirement plan at work.

▲ Invest in a reputable no-load mutual fund.

▲ Invest in companies which permit you to reinvest with the dividends that are earned.

▲ Don't take out interest and dividends earned; reinvest again.

▲ Invest in annuities that are tax-deferred until they come due. Then reinvest.

▲ Purchase rental income on a regular basis.

▲ Interview and select a good investment counselor who will assist you in these areas if you are a beginner.

This principle of saving little by little helps develop good Christian character qualities of diligence, industry, prudence, and patience.

A small amount set aside regularly grows faster (even at modest compound interest rates) than the average person realizes. If you set aside $1000 at the beginning of each year, in 20 years it will have grown substantially.

$1000 Per Year Compounded

Rate of Interest	10 years	15 years	20 years
6%	13,972	24,673	38,993
7%	14,784	26,888	43,865
8%	15,645	29,324	49,423

Secret 3:
Share Your Blessings

If we live within the basic principles which we have discussed, we will be able to share with others a part of what God has so richly given us. We can:

▲ Give to our local church.

▲ Give to other parachurch organizations (Wycliffe Translators, Billy Graham Association, Campus Crusade for Christ, etc.).

▲ Give to local community needs (Red Cross, American Cancer Association, March of Dimes, etc.).

▲ Give to individuals we meet who have needs.

▲ Give to specific interests when needs arrive (summer camp, choir tour, new piano for church, new songbooks, a short-term missionary tour, etc.).

Secret 4: Stay Out of Debt

Our advertising industry, along with manufacturers of products, have conditioned us to buy, buy, buy. We are consumers, and the economic policy which stimulates this mindset is *consumerism.* Romans 12:2 comes to mind again, because we truly are in a war of either conforming to the world system or being transformed by the renewing of our minds.

The way most of us can get there "bigger than life" is to charge it on our credit cards. Since our culture says, "The man who dies with the most toys wins," we have to discipline ourselves not to go into more debt than we can afford with our present income.

In Secret 2 we talked about saving. Debt is the very opposite of that: in life we either earn interest or pay interest. In debt we have to pay back even when we can't afford to do so. Then the collection fees become an even greater burden to us.

The wisdom of Proverbs speaks specifically about this Secret:

▲ Better is he who is lightly esteemed and has a servant than he who honors himself and lacks bread (Proverbs 12:9).

▲ There is one who pretends to be rich, but has nothing; another pretends to be poor, but has great wealth (Proverbs 13:7).

Credit cards are the "genie in the glass bottle" which lets us enter into the world of make-believe. They let us buy products we can't afford. I'm not saying that everything should be paid by cash, but I'm warning that improper use of debt will prevent us from managing our money properly. We will not be financially free as long as the monster of debt controls our lives.

The remedy for overuse of credit cards:

▲ Use your credit card to your advantage, and not to that of the lender.

▲ Pay off the balance at the end of each statement.

▲ If you're behind at the moment, stop using your card at once.

▲ On large items wait 24 hours before purchasing.

▲ Never purchase a large item on the same day that you have an impulse to do so.

▲ Use only one credit card for all expenses. Stay within your credit line. Use this card for emergencies, for car rentals, when traveling to minimize the risks of carrying cash, and as proof of purchase records, expense accounts, IRS receipt of purchase, etc.

▲ Place your credit card in your safety deposit box. It takes away the impulse to use it irresponsibly.

▲ Freeze your credit card in a container in your freezer. You can't purchase until the ice thaws.

▲ Cut up your cards if you can't manage them.

Give these four secrets a try:

▲ Earn little by little.

▲ Save little by little.

▲ Share your blessings with others.

▲ Stay out of debt.

Good Money Management Is Imperative

$ $

F or the Christian family, good money management is imperative for at least three reasons.

First, God associates our ability to handle money with our spiri-
tuality. In Luke 16:11 Jesus stated, "If you have not been trustworthy
in handling worldly wealth, who will trust you with true riches?"
(NIV). If we want to grow in spiritual responsibility and blessing, we
must prove our faithfulness in the area of financial responsibility.
God is not going to trust us spiritually if we have been irresponsible
with our money.

Second, financial responsibility is important because we are only
caretakers of what really belongs to God. Psalm 24:1 declares, "The
earth is the Lord's, and all it contains." You may possess many
things—home, car, furniture, boat, money—but you don't own
anything. Even your ability to earn money comes from God (see
Deuteronomy 8:17,18). Everything belongs to Him; you are merely a
steward of His property. God holds you personally responsible to
faithfully manage for Him whatever money or possessions He allows
you to have.

Often we are tempted to grasp our possessions selfishly as if they
belonged to us and not to God.

As caretakers of God's money and property we must obediently
grow and nurture the spiritual fruit of self-control (see Galatians
5:22,23). Every couple we have counseled over the years regarding
money problems had at least one member who lacked self-control.
Money problems were just one of many undisciplined areas in their
lives, including maintenance of the home, yard, automobile, spiritual life, personal hygiene, children, and on and on. These couples

exemplify the "easy come, easy go" generation. They are irresponsible with their money and possessions and consequently always have problems in these areas. God wants to give to us abundantly, but He also wants us to exercise self-control over the management of what He gives.

Third, financial responsibility is necessary to help us avoid a number of major money mistakes. Most couples fall into one or more of the following traps because they have not appropriated biblically based principles for the use of their money and possessions.

1. Getting into debt beyond our means to repay. We live in the now generation, and we don't like to save for something when we can buy it right now on credit. But easily available credit can become a problem when we have no predetermined limits and guidelines for spending. I am not saying that we should never go into debt, but rather that undisciplined credit spending is a big mistake (see Romans 13:8).

2. Living a money-centered life. It is easy in our culture to get caught up in the pursuit of wealth and material possessions. But Scriptures like Matthew 6:19-24 and 1 Timothy 6:6-10 warn us that *God* is to be our focus, not money. Without careful, prayerful money management we can be overly influenced by our money-centered society.

3. Trying to get rich quick. Once a reputable Christian man in our church urged me to buy some stock at $26 per share, promising me it could be sold at $40 per share within a month. I eagerly invested a large sum of money, only to lose it all when the "surefire" company went bankrupt. My overeagerness to make a financial killing cost us dearly. Proper money management will help you keep tantalizing schemes like these in perspective (see Proverbs 28:22).

4. Withholding benevolence. According to Proverbs 11:24,25, if we give generously to God and others, we will receive everything we need. But we often turn that principle around by grabbing and holding onto everything we need and want, and giving only from the leftovers—if there are any. For the Christian, being a grabber instead of a giver is not only unscriptural, but it is financially unprofitable.

5. Using people. When money becomes a high priority in our lives, our relationships often suffer. We use people as stepping-stones to promotions or personal gain, or we see people as our customers instead of those we are to love, honor, and care for. We are in trouble when we scramble the saying "Love people and use things" to read "Use people and love things."

6. Misplacing priorities. When we overemphasize money in our lives, we try to beat God's system and do things our own way. The order of the big three priorities in life—God, family, and work—often gets wrongly aligned to read—

Work, family, God
or
Work, God, family
or
Family, work, God
or
Family, God, work
or
God, work, family
until we finally get it right:
God, family, work.

At one point in my working experience I had to ask myself this very basic question: How much of my soul am I going to sell to my boss? Until I answered "no more," I was never satisfied because I was letting other people establish my priorities. When I took control of my life, I established the order of the big three in my life. Only when it was God first, family second, and work third was I really content in my job.

Principles for Financial Responsibility

Financial responsibility for Christian families can be categorized into three distinct actions: giving, receiving, and spending. When we discover God's principles for these three areas, and implement His principles with practical strategies, our needs will be met and our families blessed. Let's look closely at each area.[1]

Giving

In Chapter 9 we provided a basic overview of Christian giving. You might want to reread this chapter to refresh your mind. Just remember that everything is from God and that we are to have thankful hearts. We give back to God what He has so freely given to us.

It is amazing that we must learn to give before we receive. In the world system it is just the opposite: Receive first, then you may give.

Receiving

As giving Christians, we receive from several sources:

▲ From others giving to us (1 Corinthians 9:11)

▲ From diligent work (Genesis 3:19; 1 Thessalonians 4:11,12; 2 Thessalonians 3:10-13)

▲ From creative endeavors (Proverbs 31:13,24)

▲ From answers to prayer (Philippians 4:6; James 4:2)

Emilie and I know a couple in Newport Beach who once suffered serious financial problems because the husband was having difficulty finding a job. About ten couples from their church banded together to cover their house payments, food, insurance premiums, car expenses, and household needs while the man was out of work. The couple had always been faithful givers; this was their opportunity to receive. Like them, you may be surprised at times to see how God provides for your needs through the giving of others.

A primary way we receive is in return for our own hard work. With all the government programs for the needy today, sometimes we are tempted to look for a handout instead of a job. But Paul clearly confronted that attitude when he wrote, "He who does not work shall not eat" (2 Thessalonians 3:10 TLB). Your diligence as a worker is an avenue by which God will bless you and meet your needs.

Like the Proverbs 31 woman, couples may sometimes receive supplementary income from their creative endeavors, such as sewing, ironing, typing, woodworking, painting, or baking. Others may have the resources to open a business in their home, such as selling and distributing cosmetics, cleaning supplies, kitchenware, or nutrition items. Maybe you also have a God-given talent that you can use for extra income.

James wrote, "The reason you don't have what you want is that you don't ask God for it" (James 4:2 TLB). Since God owns everything we need, He is the ultimate source of everything we receive. We must ask Him to supply our needs, whether a certain salary, a refrigerator, or a larger home. As we present our needs to Him, He may supply them through the giving of others, a temporary job or overtime, or a completely unknown source. But we must pray to Him and expect from Him because He is our source.

In Mark 10:29,30 Jesus teaches that if we leave houses, farms, and relatives for his sake, we will receive a hundred times as much as we give up. We have proved that this principle works. We have homes in Newport Beach, Laguna Beach, Santa Barbara and Lake Arrowhead, and vacation homes in Scottsdale, Arizona; Chicago; and Stockbridge, Massachusetts. We have boats at the ocean and private jet planes. These assets didn't cost us one dime. They are at our disposal because they belong to Christian friends who give to us freely because somehow we have touched their lives along the way.

Spending

On the topic of spending, we first need to talk about *spendable income*. When you receive your paycheck, there is a very important number on it called *gross income*, the amount of money you earned before deductions. In order to figure your spendable income you need to deduct two standard expenses from your gross income.

First, you must deduct your giving to God—10 percent, for example. During a session at one of our seminars a man asked if giving should be figured on the gross or the net. A pastor in the group retorted, "Do you want to get blessed on the gross or the net?" Good point. If you are giving a percentage of your true earnings, you must figure your giving on gross income. When you consider your giving a standard expense which is taken off the top of your earnings, you will be more faithful than if you consider it an option.

Second, you must deduct local, state, and federal income taxes, approximately 15 to 35 percent, including Social Security. (Other deductions from gross income, such as medical, dental, or life insurance premiums, credit union payments, payroll savings, retirement contributions, annuities, etc. are figured elsewhere in your spending.) These two deductions equal approximately 25 to 45 percent, and the 75 to 55 percent which remains we call *spendable income*. Your spendable income is the amount you have the most control over.

Some Christian financial advisers suggest that spendable income be allocated according to the 10-70-20 plan. According to this plan, 10 percent of your spendable income should be reserved for savings and investments, including any deductions from your paycheck for these purposes.

General living expenses should be confined to 70 percent of your spendable income. This category includes all of the following:

Housing. Housing consists of all expenses necessary to operate the home, including mortgage/rent, property taxes, insurance, maintenance, and utilities. When budgeting utilities, be sure to average your payments over a 12-month period.

Food. Include all groceries, paper goods, and nonfood products normally purchased at a grocery store. Include items like bread and milk which are often purchased in between regular shopping trips. Do not include lunches or dinners at restaurants, which is another category. If you do not know your actual food expenses, keep a detailed spending record for 30 to 45 days.

Transportation. In this category include car payments, auto insurance, gas and oil, licenses, maintenance, etc. Another transportation expense is for depreciation, setting aside money to repair and/or replace your automobile. The minimum amount set aside should be enough to keep the car in decent repair, and then to replace it every four or five years. If replacement funds are not available in the budget, the minimum amount set aside should cover maintenance costs.

Annual or semiannual auto insurance premiums should be set aside monthly to avoid the crisis of a neglected expense. If you ride a bus or train to work, fares should be budgeted in this category.

Insurance. Include health, life, and disability not categorized under housing or transportation. Also include amounts deducted from your paycheck for these items.

Entertainment and recreation. Include vacations, camping trips, dining out, club dues, sporting equipment, hobby expenses, and athletic events. Don't forget Little League and booster club expenses, etc. The only effective method to budget for entertainment and recreation is to decide on a reasonable amount for your family and stay within it.

Clothing. Determine your monthly budget in this area by dividing a year's worth of expenditures by 12. The minimum amount should be $10 per family member per month.

Medical. Include insurance deductibles, doctor bills, eyeglasses, prescriptions, over-the-counter medicines, orthodontia, etc.

Miscellaneous. This category is a general catchall for items like childcare expenses for working mothers, private education costs, allowances, laundry expenses, gifts, etc.

The final 20 percent of your spendable income should be earmarked for payment of debts (loans, notes, credit cards, etc.) and emergencies. Sometimes called a buffer or margin, this amount consists of any money left over after expenses. Most couples with financial difficulty will not have any money in this account. Those who include a margin account in their budgets find it to be a helpful fund for special projects, offerings, gifts, additional savings, or future education expenses.

For every $1000 earned per month, your 10-70-20 figures would look like this:

Total income	$1000
Less giving (10%)	100
Less taxes (15-35%)	280
Total spendable income	$ 620
10% savings and investments	62
70% living expenses	434
20% debts or buffer	124

May each of us, with God's help, be good stewards of all His riches. May God say to us as He did to the servant, "Well done, good and faithful slave; you were faithful with a few things, I will put you in charge of many things; enter into the joy of your master" (Matthew 25:21).

Monthly Income and Expense Worksheet

———————— *INCOME* ————————

Gross Income (monthly)

Salary	_____
Interest	_____
Dividends	_____
Notes	_____
Rents	_____
Other	_____
TOTAL GROSS INCOME	_____

Standard Expenses

Giving to God (10%)	_____
Income taxes (15-35%)	_____
TOTAL STANDARD EXPENSES	_____

Spendable Income

(Gross income less standard expenses)   _____

———————————— *EXPENSES* ————————————

Savings and Investments (10%)

Savings _____

Investments _____

TOTAL SAVINGS & INVESTMENTS _____

Living Expenses (70%)

Housing _____

    Mortgage/rent _____

    Insurance _____

    Property taxes _____

    Electricity _____

    Gas _____

    Water _____

    Sanitation _____

    Telephone _____

    Maintenance _____

    Other _____

    TOTAL HOUSING _____

Food _____

Transportation

    Payments _____

    Gas/oil _____

    Insurance _____

    Licenses _____

Taxes _____

Maintenance _____

Other _____

TOTAL TRANSPORTATION _____

Insurance

Life _____

Medical _____

Other _____

TOTAL INSURANCE _____

Entertainment and recreation

Eating out _____

Amusements _____

Babysitters _____

Vacation _____

TOTAL ENTERTAINMENT
& RECREATION _____

Clothing _____

Medical

Doctors _____

Dentists _____

Prescriptions _____

Other _____

TOTAL MEDICAL _____

Miscellaneous

    Toiletries/cosmetics   _____

    Beauty/hair care   _____

    Laundry/cleaning   _____

    Allowances/lunches   _____

    Subscriptions   _____

    Gifts (incl. Christmas)   _____

    Sanitation   _____

    Telephone   _____

    Maintenance   _____

    Other   _____

    TOTAL
    MISCELLANEOUS   _____

Total Living Expenses   _____

Debts and Emergencies (20%)

    Credit card payment   _____

    _____

    _____

    _____

    Loan and note
    payments   _____

    Emergencies   _____

    Other   _____

    TOTAL DEBTS AND
    EMERGENCIES   _____

_____ *INCOME VERSUS EXPENSES* _____

Total Spendable Income _____

Total Expenses (10-70-20) _____

Monthly Bottom Line (income less expenses) _____

If income exceeds expenses, where will you direct your surplus income?

    1. _____

    2. _____

    3. _____

If expenses exceed income, where will you increase income?

    1. _____

    2. _____

    3. _____

If expenses exceed income, where will you cut expenses?

    1. _____

    2. _____

    3. _____

Organized for Action

▲ ▲ ▲

14

 # Create a System for Records

Money is nothing more than a resource, and money management is nothing more than a tool to use that resource.

—Ron Blue

You can have the most elaborate set of goals and a very defined set of Christian principles regarding money, but if you don't properly store your records, you will be ineffective in your overall money management program.

In the last six years we have been audited by the IRS three times. If we did not have a good record-keeping system it would have cost us a lot of time, stress, and money. (The stress is sometimes more of a factor than the other two aspects.)

The IRS auditor was very impressed with our system because with every schedule she wanted answers to, we were able to furnish the records and data to back up our figures. After a short period of time she commented favorably on our record system and the audit was completed much sooner than she anticipated. In one of the audits we had to make a minor adjustment, but on the other two audits we had no adjustments. Without the proper system I would have had major adjustments, plus it would have cost us added money for having our CPA present at $60 an hour.

By creating a simple records system you can organize your important papers in a few hours and then spend a minimum amount of time and effort staying on top of the system.

In several of her previous books Emilie talks about different aspects of record-keeping. This section will be geared to the financial aspects of your record-keeping.

You might be the kind of person who shoots from the hip and has a "sorta system." However, this system is like having no system at all. There are various reasons to have a good record system:

▲ You have total control of your financial life.

▲ You enjoy a savings in time, stress, and money.

▲ You have records to check your progress toward your financial goals.

▲ You can support your insurance claims when losses occur.

▲ You can prove payment when a vendor states he never received payment.

▲ You can support a claim if a lawsuit ever occurs.

▲ You can support your IRS and other legal claims.

▲ You have service warranties and proof of payment for previous services performed.

▲ You have easy access to documents for credit, loan, or refinancing applications.

A good system is fairly simple and doesn't take as much time to establish and maintain as most people think. What peace of mind to know where to find a particular piece of information! With the advent of millions of home personal computers, much of the paper figures can be translated to your own database. However, there are also times when you personally have to produce the original documents.

Creating a Workspace

Find some place in your home or office which you can call your own. You need either a temporary or a permanent workspace—a desk or tabletop and some form of filing cabinet. It need not be fancy or elaborate. (See Emilie's books *More Hours in My Day* or *Survival for Busy Women* to get added information on this aspect of record-keeping.)

In creating your system you will need to:

▲ Purchase an inexpensive printing calculator.

▲ Purchase at least a two-drawer file cabinet if you don't already have one.

▲ Use the top drawer to store your *transitory files*. That would include this year's receipts, bills, statements, personal papers, contracts, and agreements which are still in force.

▲ Use the bottom drawer to store your *permanent files* for previous years' papers, completed contracts, old tax returns and records, etc. You will refer to your history file only occasionally, but when you need past records, you will want them quickly. (See the end of this chapter to see how we store past IRS records.)

▲ Purchase at least 50 letter-size Manila file folders.

Deciding how long to retain transitory records can be difficult because often you don't know how long you'll need them. As a rule of thumb we suggest that you keep all employee records until you leave the job. Other transitory records you want to keep for three to five years include receipts for any major purchases you have made (jewelry, autos, art, stock certificates), plus all tax returns and all receipts for health insurance policies, credit union membership, and company stock ownership plans. Canceled checks not relating directly to specifics like home improvements should be kept for a minimum of three years in case of a tax audit. However, I usually keep these five to six years just to make sure I'm not throwing away any records I might need on a tax audit.

Your tax return, wage statements, and other papers supporting your income and deductions should be kept at least three years (that's the IRS statute of limitations for examining your return). I retain our records six years because the IRS has the right to audit within six years if they believe you omitted an item accounting for more than 25 percent of your reported income, or indefinitely if they believe you committed fraud.

Storing IRS Files

If you are familiar with Emilie's "Total Mess to Total Rest" program, you are aware of her "perfect boxes" and her numbering system of these boxes. We reserve the 15 block of numbers to store all our records pertaining to April 15. We mark them 15, 15A, 15B, 15C, 15D, 15E, etc. In box 15 we store all our past IRS and California state tax forms, and these are filed by year: 1989, 1990, 1991, 1992, etc. The other boxes we use to store various years' documents along with all the backup receipts for that year. For example, the boxes would be marked:

▲ 15A

▲ 15B

▲ 15C

▲ 15D

On a separate 3x5 card we write:

▲ 15A—1989 tax returns

▲ 15B—1990 tax returns

▲ 15C—1991 tax returns

▲ 15D—1992 tax returns

We use one card for each box. I store these 3x5 cards in an appropriate-size 3x5 file box. When I need to look through a certain year's records, I go to my file box in the 15 series and find the year. Suppose it is 1990 returns. I see that it is stored in box 15B. I go to box 15B, flip the lid up, and find all the information I need.

If I have more material than fits in one box, I reserve two or three boxes for the same year and my card would read:

▲ 15A, 15B—1990 tax returns

Every year I review my boxes that house the records that are over six years old. I consolidate my reporting forms to box 15 along with any backup data on home purchases, stock purchases, etc. that have continued tax implications. The other receipts I toss, and I can use the empty box for this year's records.

Suggested Categories for Your System

Here is a suggested checklist[1] to begin your filing system. Check those file names you can use. Add to this list any other files you will need. The name of the file folder is shown first. The items that go in the file are shown second.

_____ **Asset management account**—monthly statements, prospectuses

_____ **Bank account**—monthly statements, correspondence

_____ **Children's file**—school papers, birthday and Christmas cards, drawings, awards, diplomas, certificates

_____ **Clubs**—health club, country club, business club

_____ **Credit bureau report**

_____ **Credit card bills/receipts** (one file for each)— monthly statement and phone numbers
Enter names of each credit card you have:

_____   _____

_____   _____

_____   _____

_____ **Doctor and hospital bills**—family doctor, address, phone number, medical records, doctor and hospital bills

_____ **Education**—night school, correspondence school, work-related courses

_____ **Employment records**—employment contract, employee handbook, employee benefits information, retirement plan information

_____ **Financial blueprints**—your goals list created in Chapter 8

_____ **Guarantees, warranties, instructions**—instructions and guarantees for carpets, tires, stereo equipment, appliances, etc.

_____ **Home**—purchase contract, mortgage papers, home improvement receipts, leases and rental agreements, payment book, canceled checks

_____ **Home improvements**—records and receipts of any home improvements

_____ **Important papers**—birth certificates, marriage license number, passports, diplomas

_____ **Insurance, auto**—automobile insurance policy, traffic infractions and accidents, automobile title, driver's license number, license plate information

_____ **Insurance, health**—health insurance policy

_____ **Insurance, homeowner's**—homeowner's or tenant's insurance policy, umbrella liability policy, personal property inventory list

_____ **Insurance, life**—life insurance policies, correspondence with company, insurance quotes

_____ **Investments, annuities**

_____ **Investments, IRA accounts, Keogh accounts**

_____ **Investments, miscellaneous**—tax-sheltered annuities, savings accounts, loans to others, IOU's

_____ **Investments, mutual funds**—monthly statements, correspondence

_____ **Investments, real estate**

_____ **Investments, stock and bond certificates**

_____ **Personal**—cards, letters, pictures, etc.

_____ **Receipts**—miscellaneous

_____ **Resume**

_____ **Retirement plan**—papers relating to your employment or small-business retirement plan

_____ **Taxes, federal and state**—tax-deductible receipts,
tax returns and files for last three to seven years (see
Chapter 14)

_____ **Telephone**—telephone bills and correspondence

_____ **Utilities**—electric, gas, water, sewer bills

_____ **Will**—copy

The time required to set up and maintain these files is not
great, and it will be a great investment of your energy.

$ Setting Up a Desk and Work Area $

A wise man thinks ahead; a fool doesn't, and even brags about it.

—Proverbs 13:16 TLB

As I began to get my home in order and to eliminate all the clutter I soon realized that I didn't have an area to handle all the mail and literature that came into our home. We have had several mottos to help us focus on our home organization.

One was, **"Don't put it down, put it away."** Much of our clutter was little piles of materials that needed to be put away but we just temporarily put it down until we could put it where it belonged. At the end of the day we had piles sitting all around the home. Now we take it back to where we found it. It's amazing how the piles have disappeared!

Another motto was, **"Don't pile it, file it!"** Somewhere in the corner of the home we had piles of literature that were in no organized order. In our new program we have taken Manila folders and given them one-word headings such as **Insurance, Car, Home, Foods, Patio, Children, Utilities, Taxes.** Now we file, not pile, our papers. (See suggested headings in Chapter 15.)

During all this change in our home we still had no central desk or work area. Yet we realized we needed one in order to function properly with maximum efficiency.

Efficient paper-handling requires a good physical setting with a practical location furnished with a comfortable working surface and a good inventory of supplies. Ideally, this office will become a permanent fixture where the business life of your home is done. It should have all necessary supplies and files and should be located where other household operations do not interfere. However, if your desk/work area can't be this ideal, don't let this fact stop you from getting started. Your desk might have to be portable, but that's okay—just get started.

Since a desk or work area is so basic to a well-functioning lifestyle, we will give you some practical steps in setting up this area in your home.

Choosing the Location

The selection of your office area depends on how long you spend in your office daily. If you have a business out of your home you need to use different criteria in selecting that special site from the person who needs a place to open mail, answer mail, pay bills, and file papers. Regardless of what your precise need is, you want to choose a location that agrees with your spirit. If after a short while you find you aren't using your new space, but find yourself working in the room with the big window, you might have initially selected the wrong location, one that doesn't fully meet your needs. However, it is not always practical to work in the ideal location, often there needs to be a compromise. In order to choose the proper setting, ask yourself these questions:

▲ Do I need to be in a place where it's quiet, or is it better for me to be near people?

▲ Do big windows distract me or do I like being near windows?

▲ Do I prefer a sunny room or a shaded one?

▲ Do I prefer to work in the morning or in the afternoon?

These last two questions are related because different rooms receive varying amounts of light at different times of the day.

The answers to these questions help narrow your alternatives. Walk around your home to see which areas meet your answers to the four questions. After selecting at least two locations, you might ask yourself another set of questions:

▲ Are there enough electrical outlets and telephone jacks?

▲ Is there enough space for a desk?

▲ Is this location out of the way of other household functions? If not, can they be shifted so they won't interfere with my office hours?

▲ Is the area structurally sound?

Add the answers to these questions to your previously selected alternative and narrow your possibilities down to a final selection. Do you feel good about this selection? Live with it a few days before making a final selection. Walk to and through it several times to see that it feels good. Sit down in the area and read a magazine or book. If it still feels good, then you will probably like your choice.

Don't begin tearing out walls, adding electrical outlets, moving phone jacks, or building bookcases until you're sure you've found the right location.

Selecting Desk, Equipment, and Supplies

After you have selected the location for your office, you need to sketch the floor plan and show the room dimensions. You will use this information when you want to make or select furniture for your new work area.

The Desk

Actually, all you really need is a writing surface of some type. In some cases a portable piece of plywood is all you have or need. Look around, because you may already have around your home a suitable desk or table which would fit into the dimensions of the work area.

If you find a table, it should be sturdy, high enough to write comfortably, and large enough to hold various implements on its surface.

If you can't find a desk or table in your home, buy a desk. It is an investment you won't regret. Check your local classified ads to find a good bargain. One good source is the yellow pages of your phone book under "Office Furniture—Used." You need not pay full price. Many times these stores will deliver to your home free or with a minimum charge.

You should have no trouble finding a desk which has the practical characteristics of office models but is still attractive in your home. Here are a few specifications to keep in mind.

1. Writing surface. Your desk should be sturdy and comfortable to use, with a surface that doesn't wobble.

2. Place for supplies. Have at least one large drawer in which paper and envelopes can be kept in folders. If you find a desk with large drawers on each side, so much the better. There needs to be a shallow drawer with compartments for paper clips, rubber bands, and other supplies. At your local stationery store you can purchase small trays with dividers that can store these small items.

3. Files and records. A home office seldom has need for more than one file drawer, or sometimes two. If your desk has at least one drawer big enough to contain letter-size file folders (legal size accommodation is preferable), all your files will probably be comfortably accommodated. If you can't purchase a file cabinet at this time, go back and read "Total Mess to Total Rest" in Emilie's *More Hours in My Day* or *Survival for Busy Women*, where she talks about the **Perfect Box**. These make excellent file boxes until you are able to purchase a file cabinet. Watch your newspaper for stationery "sale" offerings.

4. Typing platform. If you have a typewriter or a personal computer and plan to use it in your work area, try to get a desk with a built-in platform for these to rest on. If you have enough room in your office you might want to designate a separate area in your office for these two functions.

If you don't have enough space for a regular stationery desk in your home, look into portable storage to house your stationery and supplies. Go again to your local office supply store and have them recommend products that will service this need. You will still need a file cabinet or its short-term substitute (the Perfect Box) and a sturdy swivel chair just for the office area. (The swivel chair permits you to turn from one position to another without getting up.)

Other Storage Ideas

- ▲ Wall organizers are helpful for pads, pens, calendars, and other supplies.
- ▲ Paper, pencils, and miscellaneous supplies can be kept in stackable plastic or vinyl storage cubes kept under the desk.

▲ Use an extra bookcase shelf for portable typewriter, basket of supplies, or some files.

▲ Decorative objects (such as a ceramic mug) look attractive holding pencils and pens.

▲ Use stackable plastic bins that can be added on to for your expanded needs. Use the small style for stationery and papers, and a larger size (a vegetable bin) for magazines and newspapers.

Supplies

For your shopping convenience I have given you a checklist of supplies that you will need to stock your office. Again, try to purchase these items on sale or at an office supply discount store. Watch your local paper for these sales, or look under "Office Supplies" in the yellow pages. Many times bulk buying is the way you will get your best prices.

_____ Address book or Rolodex. I personally like both; the address book I take with me when traveling or on business, and the Rolodex I keep permanently located on my desk. The Rolodex has room for adding other information you might want to use when addressing that particular person or business.

_____ Appointment calendar. Ideally the calendar should be small enough to carry around with your notebook, as well as to use at your desk. If you search around, you can find a combination notebook and calendar that isn't too bulky to carry around in your briefcase or purse. The date squares should be large enough to list appointments comfortably. In our "Working Woman's Seminars" we offer an excellent organizer called "Harper House/Day Runner." This product does an excellent job in meeting this need.

_____ Bulletin board. This is a good place to collect notes and reminders to yourself. Attach notes with pushpins.

_____ Business cards. A must time-saver.

_____ Carbon paper. Make a carbon copy of every business letter you write. Your office supply store can help you with this selection. Every year new formats come on the market.

———— Computer, desktop. You will need to shop around for this tool if you are inclined to incorporate this in your money management system.

———— Desk lamp. A three-way bulb will give you a choice of light levels.

———— Dictionary and/or electronic speller.

———— File folders. I use colored "third-cut" folders in which the tabs are staggered so they don't block each other from view. The colors give a more attractive appearance to your file drawer.

———— Letter opener.

———— Marking pens. I keep on hand a few marking pens in different colors. (I do a lot of color-coding on my calendar.) I also use the "yellow hi-lite" when I want some information to pop out at me for rereading.

———— Paper clips. Regular and large.

———— Postcards. These save money on your mailing.

———— Pencil sharpener. If you use a lot of pencils, I recommend a desktop electric model.

———— Pencils and pens.

———— Postage scale. A small inexpensive type.

———— Rubber bands. Mixed sizes.

———— Rubber stamp and ink pad. There are all kinds of rubber stamps you can use in your office. These are much cheaper than printed stationery or labels. If you use a certain one over and over, you might consider having a self-inking stamp made for you (a great time-saver).

———— Ruler.

———— Scissors.

———— Scratch paper. Use lined pads for this purpose. 3-M "Post-It-Notes" are also great for this.

———— Scotch tape and dispenser.

———— Stamps. In addition to regular stamps, keep appropriate postage on hand for additional weight and special handling.

———— Stapler, staples, staple remover. If you do a lot of stapling you might consider an electric model (saves time and the palm of your hand).

_____ Stationery and envelopes. Usually the 8½ x 11 plain white paper (with matching business-size envelopes) is all you will need. If you use a printed letterhead stationery you will need to get some plain white or matching colored second sheets. I find that 9x6 and 9x12 Manila envelopes are good for mailing bulk documents, books, or magazines. Sometimes a #6 Jiffy padded envelope can be used to ship items that need some protection from rough handling in transit.

_____ Telephone. An extension right at your desk is great. I use my cordless telephone for this purpose and it works just fine.

_____ Typewriter.

_____ Typewriter correction fluid or paper.

_____ Wastebasket.

You now have an office space that lets you function to your maximum ability. This addition to your lifestyle will make you more efficient in other areas of your life, and it will give you a special feeling of accomplishment.

$ Me? Balance a $ Checkbook?

The one dreaded chore that we all have to face is balancing a checkbook. Unless God has gifted you with special strengths, you find that this monthly exercise is not a great deal of fun. Yet I find this to be one of the important exercises in money management. In our home, Emilie takes care of all the banking for our family expenses and I manage all the finances relating to More Hours in My Day. She balances her checkbook and I balance the business checking account and books.

An absolute rule in our home is to reconcile the bank statements within 48 hours of receiving them. Keeping these up-to-date is very, very important!

There are several ways to maintain a proper record of the checks. They are:

▲ Store them in the Manila file folder labeled "Bank Account."
▲ Store them in a separate check file box intended just for canceled checks.
▲ File checks in order by check number, along with deposit slips, deposit receipts, and your check register.
▲ Don't leave canceled checks and statements lying loose in a drawer.
▲ Don't assume that your statement is accurate just because it is mechanically done. Errors can be made.

Reconcile each monthly statement by using the form found on the back of your statement. If the check is for an item that is tax deductible at the end of the year, I make a copy of this check and file it in my "Taxes" Manila folder. If you don't have access to a copy machine, you can put a red "T" in the upper-right-hand corner of the check for ease in documenting at tax time. At tax time I have quick access to a copy of these and can make quick calculations for our federal and state tax returns. I also photocopy all checks which I need for future verification of major purchases, stock purchases, and contract agreements. I staple this copy to the original document.

The steps in reconciling your bank statements are:

1. Be certain all your deposits were recorded correctly. Compare your deposit receipts with the deposit entries on your statement.

2. Be certain the correct check amounts are deducted from your bank balance. Compare each check returned in your statement envelope to the amount deducted by the bank on your statement. Anything that doesn't agree is a bank error.

3. Identify checks outstanding that have not been deducted from your account. Just check off with a red pen in your check register all checks returned with your statement. Any check register entries not marked are checks you have written that were not received by the bank by the time your statement was prepared. These outstanding checks must be deducted from the balance shown on your statement to determine the actual balance in your account at the present time.

4. Identify and deduct bank charges. Your bank will charge you for anything it can, including NSF (nonsufficient funds) checks, ATM usage, or a minimum monthly account charge. Deduct the total of these charges (once you are certain they are correct) in your check register to adjust your actual balance. By the same token, add any amounts credited to you for interest-bearing accounts and/or deposits which you have made after the statement date.

5. Contact your bank immediately if you find any errors in your account.

You should never have to call your bank to find out what your balance is. If you reconcile each statement you will *know* what your balance is.

Balancing Your Checking Account

Before you start, be sure you have entered all transactions **in your checkbook**, including interest earned, electronic activity, and bank charges as shown on your statement.

A. Enter Deposits **not shown on this statement** (including electronic).

Date of Deposit	Amount
_____	_____
_____	_____
_____	_____
Total A	$ _____

B. Enter all checks, all withdrawals (including electronic) and any bank charges **not shown on this statement**.

Outstanding Item/Check No.	Amount
_____	_____
_____	_____
_____	_____
_____	_____
_____	_____
_____	_____

Total B	$ _____
Ending balance on your statement	$ _____
TOTAL A +	$ _____
=	$ _____
TOTAL B	$ _____
Current Balance =	$ _____

(Should equal your checkbook balance)

Have a Safe Deposit Box

$ $

Burned papers and important documents are difficult to replace. Your local bank can provide you with various sizes of deposit boxes to meet your needs. We started with the smallest box the bank had and have grown about two sizes over the years.

Many of the new homes in California come with fireproof safety storage areas. Here is a list of important, hard-to-replace papers that may be considered for safekeeping at the bank or in your deposit area at home:

- ▲ Treasury bond certificates
- ▲ Mutual fund shares
- ▲ Stock or bond certificates
- ▲ Property deeds
- ▲ Automobile titles
- ▲ Personal property inventory list and photographs
- ▲ Marriage certificate
- ▲ Will and estate plan
- ▲ Birth certificates
- ▲ Diplomas
- ▲ Military discharge papers
- ▲ Passports
- ▲ Negatives of important family photographs
- ▲ Personal property video copy

If you use a home safe, make sure it is fire-rated and that it is securely attached to the floor for added protection. Having a safe at home is much more convenient than going back and forth to the bank.

$ Review Your Spending Habits $

Have you found honey? Eat only what you need, lest you have it in excess and vomit it.

—Proverbs 25:16

I've learned that if it tastes good it's probably bad for your health. Everything that's fun seems to be either fattening, immoral, or expensive! Our family tries to be cost-conscious, but no matter how hard we shop for an item, the day after we buy it, it will go on sale!

One way you can have more funds to meet your bills is by reviewing your spending habits.

▲ Stop using your credit cards except for gasoline purchases or business expenses that will be reimbursed by your employer. Leave all bank cards, charge cards, travel cards, etc. at home.

▲ Carry only enough cash for each day's needs. There's no chance of spending money if you don't have it with you. Besides, with the crime spree in our country it isn't safe to carry excess cash.

▲ Leave your checkbook at home—again, another attempt to stop your careless spending.

▲ Shop sales. Use discipline to buy only what is on sale. Store owners many times advertise a "loss leader" to get you into their store, knowing that once you are there your sales resistance will weaken and you will buy items that aren't on sale. Say NO! Don't buy nonsale items. Listed below are the months which target specific items:

When Items Go On Sale

Item:	Likely to be on sale in:
Appliances	January, July
Bedding	January, February, August
Books	January
Cars, new	August, September
Cars, used	February, November
Clothing, summer	June, July
Clothing, winter	November, December
Linens	January, May
School supplies	August, October
Televisions	May, June
Toys	January, February

▲ Don't buy state lottery tickets. The average lottery ticket buyer spends at least $250 per year for this extravagance, but never wins anything.

▲ Drop to the next lower grade in the products you use. You can maintain the same quality by purchasing generic brand products at the supermarket.

▲ Cut back on eating out. The average American spends 37 percent of his or her food budget in restaurants. The typical restaurant price is twice what it would be at home and is usually of poorer nutritional quality because it has more fat, more sodium, more cholesterol, and more sugar. By eating at home you can better control your diet requirements.

We have found that people with poor money management have poor spending habits. Change your spending habits and you will upgrade your financial status.

PART FOUR

The Know-How for Managing Money

▲ ▲ ▲

Little Remedies for Money Headaches

Seek first His kingdom and His righteousness, and all these things shall be added to you.

—Matthew 6:33

When you have money problems, you have to be creative in trying to get back in control. Here are several ideas that can help you think creatively.

Remedy 1: Hold a garage sale. You would be amazed at how much money you have lying around your home and garage. Lump your unneeded property together and sell it all at once. Try to coordinate a combined sale with your immediate neighbors; you'll get larger attendance and the competition will actually improve sales in most cases. Use the profits to help get financial relief; don't be tempted to purchase your neighbor's stuff!

Remedy 2: Sell any major drain on your cash flow. It might be a second home, a car, a recreational vehicle, a boat, even a main home. Whatever the drain, you might want to sell that item or items until you can solve your money problems.

Remedy 3: Check your life insurance to see if you have cash value you can borrow. Take advantage of this source if available. You may even want to review all your insurance policies and make basic adjustments if you have coverage that is unnecessary. You should also consider switching any whole life to term insurance, taking your surrender value in cash and paying off your excessive debt.

Remedy 4: Go back to the basics until you get caught up. That means carrying your lunches to work, eating at McDonald's for a dinner out, walking or riding your bicycle for neighborhood errands, and making no new purchases (that includes clothes, too). This method really hurts, but is necessary to get an immediate increase in cash.

Remedy 5: Obtain a bill-payer loan. In this method you must use great discipline. The money borrowed can't be used for anything but to pay off old bills. Many people splurge when they get this loan, but you can't. As you ease the money pain, you will be tempted to go out and use this money for frills.

Remedy 6: Put your hobby to work. Many men and women are able to put their hobbies to work. We know of people who specialize in baking bread, making gourmet desserts, carving wood ducks, sewing clothing, making alterations, detailing automobiles, doing artwork, and typing papers. Many home businesses are started out of hobbies.

Remedy 7: Get an extra job. Many of our teacher friends use this skill by tutoring a few students. Accountants use their skill around tax time. If you love children you might want to babysit a few hours each day. Many parents need help before and after school hours. Working parents and single parents need housecleaning chores done so they can keep up their domestic duties. Our sister-in-law hires an elderly man to hand-water the wildflowers around her home.

Remedy 8: Use extra money to pay off debt. Tax refunds, Christmas funds, selling a car, or inheriting money from a deceased relative can be used to get you caught up. This is not as much fun as purchasing new clothes, a new car, or an expensive holiday weekend, but you must use discipline to get those bills paid.

Remedy 9: Sell any collectibles that you might have. Get an appraisal of their value and consider selling them. Many times these collectibles have become keepsakes, but when you have a debt problem, this is an area that needs consideration.

Remedy 10: Call your main creditors. Go on the offensive; don't wait for them to come to you. Creditors will appreciate you coming to them first. Many times these creditors are willing to alter their payment schedule to help you during this tight time. Most creditors don't want you to file personal bankruptcy because then they only get a fractional payment. Keeping you making payments even if it is less than they would desire is better than getting no payment at all.

> *Unless you have unlimited resources,*
> *you cannot have everything.*
> —Ron Blue

How to Get Out of Debt

Owe nothing to anyone except to love one another, for he who loves his neighbor has fulfilled the law.

—Romans 13:8

It's sad to say, but approximately 80 percent of all Americans have negative net worth (which means that they owe more than they are worth). Professional marriage counselors indicate that stress over mismanagement of money is a leading cause of the disintegration of the family unit. Debt and its related problems are the banana peel that many of us slip on. Once we are down in debt, it is very hard to get out and stay out.

When you spend more money than you make, the result is debt. Unfortunately, credit cards make it possible to go into debt very easily. You may be flooded by mail indicating that you have just been approved for X amount of dollars from company Y. What an easy way to get a loan approved! When you sign up for such a good deal, you have just become a slave of that bank.

Once you have gotten into debt, how do you get out? Below are five steps to help you out of this dilemma.

1. Recognize That There Is No Easy Way Out of Debt

It's a lot easier to get in than out. Getting out takes good planning, discipline, hard work, and time. In order to get out of debt, you must also fight the added effect of interest on the loan. You not only have to pay off the debt itself, but you also have to pay off the interest on the debt.

2. *Try to Increase Your Income*

Extra labor doesn't always increase cash flow. In fact, it is possible to work several hours overtime and have the extra taxes cause you to receive less than if you had not worked extra at all.

By following the principles listed below you can increase your cash flow.

▲ **Avoid impulse buying.** Plan ahead for the things you need to purchase, and don't buy anything that isn't on your shopping list.

▲ **Shop comparatively.** It takes a little time to find what the best price is on an item or a service, but if you do this consistently it can really make a difference in your cash flow.

▲ **Buy at the right time.** Many prices are seasonal. Buy melons in August, not January. Buy swimming suits in August, not April.

▲ **Don't stay unemployed long.** In times of recession it pays to anticipate a job layoff before it happens and to begin job-hunting before your old job expires.

▲ **Use your credit card carefully.** A credit card can be a very handy way to purchase items. However, if the account is not paid off completely each month, it can be an anesthetic used to cover the pain of debt.

▲ **Use a checking account.** If it is too difficult to discipline yourself with a credit card, destroy the card and just use a checking account. And don't write "rubber" checks!

▲ **Use banks, but don't let them use you.** Shop around for the highest rate of return on your bank accounts.

▲ **Buy quality.** Cheap goods aren't necessarily economical. In the long run, high-quality products may outlast and outperform poor-quality goods many times over.

▲ **Develop money-saving hobbies.** Many expensive services can be done by families themselves. Anything from tree trimming to plumbing can be done by handy families.

3. Begin to Pay Off Debt

By practicing cost savings techniques you should have more money to pay off your debts. Pay off the debt with the highest interest rate first, the second-highest next, and so forth.

4. Begin to Prevent Future Debt

As you pay off one debt, don't go back into debt for something else. The money you save will help you build a cushion for that rainy day. Tear up those extra credit cards that got you into trouble in the first place.

5. Dedicate Your Finances to God

Many blessings in Scripture are promised to people who dedicate their finances to God (that means assets as well as liabilities).

- ▲ After the slave invested the money his Lord said, "Well done, good and faithful slave; you were faithful with a few things, I will put you in charge of many things; enter into the joy of your master" (Matthew 25:21-23).

- ▲ Honor the Lord with your possessions, and with the first-fruits of all your increase; so shall your barns be filled with plenty, and your vats will overflow with new wine (Proverbs 3:9,10 NKJV).

- ▲ My God shall supply all your needs according to His riches in glory (Philippians 4:19).

- ▲ Instruct those who are rich in this present world not to be conceited or to fix their hope on the uncertainty of riches, but on God, who richly supplies us with all things to enjoy (1 Timothy 6:17).

Managing Your Finances in Tough Times

Where your treasure is, there will your heart be also.

—Matthew 6:21

During recessionary times, many businesses, families, and individuals struggle to keep their investments together. Though unemployment is more rampant in certain geographical regions than others, almost all Americans taste the stress of reduced income at one time or another.

Here are several ideas to be used in any economic climate, but particularly in tough times.

Idea 1: Budget Your Money

One of the hardest things to teach individuals and couples is to make a budget. They find it boring, and it gives little gratification. However, a budget is a must when we have limited income or when we lose a job.

If you don't know where your money goes every month, you probably haven't taken the time to analyze your monthly income and outgo. It is very important for you to know how much money you spend on a regular basis, and how much you owe.

For the next three months keep a diary or log of where you spend every cent (outgo) of your paycheck (income). After studying this log on a regular basis you can readily determine items that must be reduced or cut from your expenses. There are times when you must take a very sharp knife and make drastic cuts. In these situations you can't wait long; you must do it *now*. See Chapter 13 for more information on budgeting.

Idea 2: Build Up an Emergency Nest Egg

All of us must have a fund equivalent to three to six months of take-home pay to help us in case of emergencies. You might yell, "I can't do that!" I would whisper back to you, "You must if you are a manager of your money!"

If you are in a field or career that is susceptible to layoffs, seasonal ups and downs, or recessions, you should have more than six months of salary in your nest egg. You need to save at least 10 percent of your annual take-home pay for this purpose. It takes a great deal of discipline and the ability to delay gratification, but it will certainly give you a sense of well-being when an emergency hits.

Over the years we have paid ourselves first with a check to be deposited in our savings account. We also contribute regularly to our IRA plan and to a self-directed Keogh fund. Not only are these tax-deferred, but we reinvest the dividends back into additional purchases of stock. We purchase a $100 EE Treasury bond periodically at the bank and store it in our safe deposit box for safekeeping. These tools help our savings begin building for retirement.

Idea 3: Discuss Asset Management with Those You Respect

Seek out those friends whom you respect and who seem to have a handle on their finances. Question them on how they do it and what basic principles they use. Have ready your specific concerns, and write them down on paper so you will be organized when you meet with these people. This way you won't forget specific questions.

Sometimes wisdom is hard to hear, because a wise person may give you advice that is hard to take. But be receptive and not defensive when such a person gives you specifics. Be sure to write him or her a thank-you note for giving his time to you.

Idea 4: Get Rid of Your Credit Cards

If things are getting tight for you and your family, pay cash or don't buy. The last thing you need during tight times is debt, particularly credit card debt. The way business and credit is worked in America, you need at least one card in order to rent cars, verify purchases, make hotel reservations, etc., but these balances *must* be paid off at the end of each statement. If you can't do this, then don't use the card.

Watch out for credit card traps. Many banks are lowering their credit-card rates. It's about time! However, to make more money, some banks are changing the way they calculate finance charges and fees.

One trick is the so-called *two-cycle, average-daily-balance method.* Finance charges are based on outstanding balances over *two* monthly billing periods, which could hit those who don't pay bills in full each month. As a result, finance charges are doubled, wiping out any anticipated savings from a lower interest rate.

Another method banks use to boost cardholders' bills is to *include new purchases* (since the end of the last billing cycle) *when calculating the balance subject to finance charge.* This penalizes those of us who pay our bill in full and on time each month.

Two other methods of calculating finance charges are based on the *adjusted balance* (the amount outstanding at the beginning of a billing period, minus payments and credits during the period) and the *previous balance* (the balance outstanding at the beginning of the billing period).

Under federal regulations, card issuers must disclose the type of method used for finance charges, but they don't have to explain how the method works. To find out, you must call the issuer and ask how the method works. You might find that you're paying much more than you think on late charges. You can get more information from these sources:

- ▲ **RAM Research** publishes a newsletter, *CardTrak.* Call 800-344-7714.
- ▲ **Bankcard Holders of America** (Herndon, VA) puts out various consumer information brochures. Call 800-553-8025 for further information.

Idea 5: Establish a Line of Credit

Not that you are going to borrow, but to have credit approved in case of an emergency. The best source of credit that is also still tax-deductible is a home equity loan. We don't recommend this as a normal way to get funds, but your home equity can be used in an emergency.

Make sure your lender gives you a line of credit with little or no up-front charges and no interest due until you decide you need the money. Start with your bank or credit union if you have been satisfied with their service.

If not, shop around; ask others who have done the same and get recommendations from them. You may check your local newspaper or the yellow pages of your phone directory to find appropriate lending institutions.

We suggest that you consider only a fixed-rate home equity loan instead of an ARM (one with adjustable rates).

Idea 6: Keep Your Investments Liquid and Safe

When times get tough, you want to keep your investments where you can get them. You usually won't be getting the highest rate of interest, but you want to be conservative and take no risks. This can be done by having your money invested in:

▲ Money market funds

▲ CD's (short-term)

▲ Money-market mutual funds

▲ Government-guaranteed securities

A few funds to help you are:

▲ **Benham Government Agency Fund** (800-472-3389 or 415-965-4274). Minimum investment: $1000. It's as safe as any Treasury fund, but with an extra half-point or more in yield, plus tax advantages in many states. Benham is personally my top pick for yield and safety.

▲ **Scudder Short-Term Bond Fund** (800-225-2470 or 617-439-4640). Minimum investment: $1000.

▲ **Blanchard Short-Term Global Income Fund** (800-688-7904). Minimum investment: $3000.

Idea 7: Consider Starting a New Part-Time Business

What a great time to start that dream of a business you have had for so many years! Emergencies certainly lend themselves to creativity, and now is the time to look into that possibility. We know of many couples who have started businesses in their homes during this time. Many have gone into multilevel marketing products and have done very well.

The U.S. Small Business Administration (SBA) has a number of publications designed to help new businesses. These include *Checklist for Going into Business*, *Developing a Strategic Business Plan*, *Researching Your Market*, and *Goal Setting for Small Business*. To order a free directory of publications and videotapes, call the Small Business Answer Desk at 800-368-5855 or 202-653-7561 (in Washington D.C.). In the directory you will find an order form for the booklets mentioned above, plus more.

Idea 8: Develop Your Own Strategies for Smart Money Management

▲ Pay off any personal loans you have. (Those interest charges are no longer tax-deductible.)

▲ Review your W4 form. You need not overpay your taxes to Uncle Sam.

▲ Maximize your contributions to your IRA's, Keogh's, or company pension plans.

▲ Start a nest egg fund.

$ Women: Shape Up Your Financial Muscles! $

She goes out to inspect a field, and buys it; with her own hands she plants a vineyard.

—Proverbs 31:16 TLB

I n our various seminars on marriage and relationships, we point out that there are emotional, physical, and psychological differences between men and women. There are also some financial differences.

▲ Women generally underrate the value of their labor.

▲ Until recently, women have had difficulty in making certain financial transactions.

▲ Approximately 50 percent of marriages end up in divorce, with women usually getting the children and the financial burden for raising the children.

▲ Most Americans living below the poverty line are women.

Historically women's work pay scale has been less than men's. One way to break this wage restriction is to have women take jobs which have usually been held by men, such as engineers, construction workers, attorneys, doctors, truck drivers, etc.

In order to break away from the historical limitations, there are several things you can do.

1. Improve Your Financial Position—NOW!

▲ **Increase your base salary.** You may have to ask your boss for a raise, take a second job, or develop your hobby into a paying endeavor.

▲ **Create your own line of credit.** Maintain a good credit record with your telephone company, utility company, and a gasoline credit card. Make sure you have a good reference with your bank by having both a savings and a checking account. Build a good credit history by establishing a department store charge account, adding an oil company credit card if you don't have one in your name, and applying for a small loan to be backed up by your signature or collateral. These accounts are only to help you establish credit in your name. They are not to go into debt beyond your ability to pay. Great discipline must be used in developing this strategy.

▲ **Protect your principal**. Be cautious with your money and don't speculate with your investments. At this stage you want assets, not losses.

2. Improve Your Financial Self-Worth in the Workplace

Surveys show that girls rate the importance of boys' labor higher than their own. Interestingly, boys rate girls' work equal to their own. It appears that our culture has trained women to think less of their labor. However, don't underrate yourself. Begin a fair appraisal of your worth to your company. If you feel you are carrying your part in making the company profitable, you should ask for a raise, ask for a job with more responsibility with more pay, or begin to look for a better job.

3. Take Steps to Get a Pay Increase

There are certain steps you can take to do this:

▲ **Take an inventory of your good points.** Write them down on paper. Why are you valuable to your company?

▲ **Decide how much you are worth.** Do a salary survey on your own to see how much others are making in your same job.

▲ **Ask for the raise.** If you are stalled, ask again. Here are a couple of reminders of what *not* to do:

1. Don't threaten to quit. If you want to leave, just give your notice (make sure you have a new job first, if possible).

2. Don't change your mind once you have given notice.

3. Be professional and don't complain with the other employees.

4. Don't be angry, but feel good about the decision you make.

4. Take Steps to Get a Better-Paying Job

There are certain positions within a company that more directly contribute to profitability than others. Where does your job fit into contributing to that profitability? You may want to change job classifications in order to be more important to your own company or to a new company. You might want to:

▲ **Go into sales.** Direct sales of a company's product will pay you more than being a sales clerk. Executive sales pays excellently, and it's a field where more and more women excel. As long as you can sell you will be rewarded.

▲ **Get more education if needed.** Many communities have continued education in evening classes in all areas of vocation. If you don't have a bachelor of arts degree, you might want to consider enrolling in a nearby college or university.

▲ **Learn a skill that pays well.** There are many such careers available in computer works, service industry, dental and medical assistance, etc.

▲ **Start your own business.** You can start from scratch or enter into the vast field of multilevel marketing companies. This type of business will reward you according to your production.

$ Single Persons Can $
Live Without Stress

Happiness comes to those who are fair to others and are always just and good.

—Psalm 106:3 TLB

In America today we see an increasing number of people who would be counted as single. They fall into one of three categories:

▲ Those who have never been married

▲ Those who are divorced

▲ Those whose spouse has died.

The single person who has never been married is most often a young man or woman who is just getting started in the financial world. People are getting married later in life today; it is not uncommon to meet 35-year-olds still single by choice. This category of single usually doesn't have an income problem, but they do with outgo. If this is you, a few survival tips would be:

▲ **Establish income goals.** You have probably learned to live within your present income level. As a single you can do this with less adjustment than a married couple. Unfortunately, you may very well be adapting yourself to a low income by having inadequate savings, cutting back where you need not, and having insufficient money for vacations. Revise your income goals to be more challenging than what they presently are.

▲ **Have a disciplined budget.** Know what you need to spend, then be sure to allocate your income accordingly. (Refer back to Chapter 13.)

▲ **Don't buy too much life insurance.** For single people I recommend buying a good term insurance policy that covers burial costs and any other expenses that might be incurred following death.

▲ **Have an adequate health insurance program.** If you work for a company with a group health insurance policy, this will usually be adequate. If you are self-employed, you will need to seek out a good agent who will advise you of adequate coverage.

▲ **Save and invest.** See our chapters dealing with this topic. There are excellent no-load or low-load growth-type mutual funds which you can invest in through a monthly investment plan. Don't invest in risky investments, or respond from a telemarketing salesperson on the telephone. Only go with a sound, financial adviser who comes highly recommended by personal referrals.

▲ **Control your expenses.** Be very careful on your outgo of money. Many singles can get into a very damaging habit of living beyond their means through splurging on luxury items.

▲ **Have tax-deferred retirement savings.** Since most single unmarried people are young, they think retirement is too far ahead for them to think about: "I'll take care of that as I get older." You want to start *now*. Don't wait!

Living As a Divorced Person

This is the most difficult of the three single categories. In most cases both parties suffer financially, particularly if children are involved. As a man you will have to provide adequate alimony and/or child support. You will certainly need to budget as you have never done before. Without proper budgeting you will fall behind on your obligations and everyone will suffer.

As a woman you will struggle to be the single head of a household on an inadequate income, in most cases. You will need to build or rebuild your career goals. Here are a few things you can do to help the situation:

▲ Arrange a satisfactory alimony trust as part of the divorce settlement. Not everyone will have enough assets to fund this.

▲ You will not be able to maintain the same lifestyle as when you were married. Divorce always hurts financially. Both parties will usually have to cut back.

▲ Be faithful to your responsibilities. Irresponsibility in these areas will be the beginning of many legal and financial woes.

▲ Make sure there is adequate insurance to protect against disaster.

▲ Have a savings account to cover emergencies.

▲ Have a living trust or will made.

Those Whose Spouses Have Died

Insurance charts indicate that most women will live eight years longer than their husbands. You will need to carry on when he is gone, so don't wait until it's too late. Begin *today* to learn basic survival techniques for around the house:

▲ Where the electrical box is located.

▲ Where to turn off the gas and water.

▲ Where the list is of the repairmen.

▲ The location of savings and investments.

▲ Who handles the insurance policies.

▲ A review of monthly payments.

▲ Basic repair skills to avoid having expensive repairmen come.

There are scores of details that must be handled before the surviving spouse can carry on a normal daily routine. You might want to start a log to answer all these questions.

The largest percentage of Americans living below the poverty level are widows. Review your insurance and retirement benefits so you will have a basic understanding of your resources that will carry you through your remaining years.

Living Alone

Here are some helpful hints that will help you live alone:

▲ Learn to live economically. Protect your savings and retirement funds. If you work, continue to save if possible.

▲ Use all the resources that you are eligible for. Since you qualify, don't hesitate to use whatever benefits you have coming to you.

▲ Maintain your health insurance. As you get older, this is one of your most important coverages. Insure for the disaster.

▲ Have adequate life insurance coverage to pay for your final illness and burial expenses.

▲ If you have spare bedrooms, you might want to look around for someone to live with you. This income will help offset your expenses and will help you from becoming lonely.

▲ Continue working if you can. Even part-time work helps financially, plus it keeps you involved creatively.

▲ Have a current living trust or will made.

$ You Need to Be $ Bank Savvy

Consumers need to be savvy in their use of banking services. Usually we just experience these services, but we don't take the time to sit down with an officer of the bank and ask questions which will help us to make wise financial decisions.

Consider these ideas in order to become more savvy:

1. Ask your bank for a loan on a simple-interest-payment note. This allows for monthly repayments or an installment loan figured on a simple-interest basis. You are charged interest on the balance outstanding at any point in time. On just a modest loan of a few thousand dollars you can save hundreds of dollars in the process. Some banks say they don't have this type of loan to consumers, but just for businesses. However, shop around and ask the questions anyway.

2. Stay away from credit life and disability insurance from the bank. This type of insurance is designed to pay off debt in the event that the borrower dies before the loan is paid off. You can get better terms from an independent insurance company.

3. Get to know an officer at your branch bank. It's always good to know the manager and several tellers on a first-name basis. Then if you need VIP treatment, a loan, or an out-of-town check cashed, you're more likely to get efficient assistance.

4. Rethink having a safe deposit box at your bank. Bank safe deposit boxes may not be as safe as you have been led to believe. They can be broken into, have fires, or fall to floods and other disasters. Ask if your contents are insured if such things happen. One other negative consideration is that the IRS or state government agencies can get a warrant to invade your box and confiscate its contents to pay their claims. In this case the banks must comply. One solution in which you have more control and where the long-range cost is cheaper is to buy a home safe that meets or exceeds the fire rating of your bank vault. The approximate cost of such a home vault is about $250. Look in the local yellow pages to locate your nearest safe sales store. (Your home insurance policy can cover the contents, if you properly document the contents.)

5. Automatic Teller Machines (ATM's) aren't for everyone. When this service was first introduced to the public it replaced drive-up window service and was introduced to give 24-hour service, at the same time eliminating the labor cost of this service. However, many banks now charge for this service. ATM's have become a profit center for a lot of banks. These machines have also caused an increase in crime. Most banks do not provide security guards for their customers. If you must use ATM's, exercise common sense. Make sure it's not late at night and that there is adequate lighting in the evening; have someone accompany you to the bank; make sure there is other traffic in the area.

6. Be alert to the proper use of overdraft protection. If you aren't careful this becomes just another credit card. You can get into financial trouble very quickly and end up paying excessive amounts of interest for the money advanced. This service is designed to keep you from bouncing checks (which creates fear and added embarrassment and charges). Talk to your bank official to properly understand what the service is and how much it costs.

One way to minimize this cost is to have your bank "red tag" your account and call you when you don't have enough money in your account to pay for an outstanding check. Then you can go to the bank and make a deposit to cover the amount of the check without paying any overdraft fee.

7. Shop before taking out a mortgage. Banking is very competitive, and it will pay you to shop for the best loan possible. A savings on points and interest rate will result in long-range profits for you. A 1 percent reduction on a $100,000, 30-year, 9 percent loan will save you about $25,000; a 1/2 percent cut will reduce your costs about half that amount. Start with your local bank, but if they won't budge, move on to another bank. You will probably find someone who can give you a big savings. It will certainly be worth your extra effort.

8. Paying off the principal on your mortgage might make sense. This is a debatable topic, since different financial planners have varying ideas on this matter. However, we are strong advocates of this idea. For almost eight years we have sent in with our monthly payment an additional sum of money (based on what we have available for this strategy). By simply increasing your monthly payment by a modest amount, and/or by making your payments early, you will be able to shorten the repayment term significantly, which will lower your total costs.

If you have a $100,000, 30-year mortgage at $9^{1}/_{2}$ percent, with a monthly payment of $840.85, you will have a total repayment of $302,707.51 over the life of the loan. By adding just $50 per month to your regular payments, you will repay that 30-year loan in just 23 years and three months. The biggest factor is that you will save over $54,000.

9. Stay away from bank escrow funds for your home insurance and property taxes. Why not draw your own interest from these funds rather than having them accrue in a non-interest-bearing account? You want to be in control of this money. In some cases you will have to shop around to have this ability. Tell your bank you will not agree to an escrow account unless it pays a fair-market interest rate on your funds in that account.

These nine considerations are worth money in your pocket. Don't be timid in asking for considerations from your bank. Remember, you are the customer.

How to Be a Saver

The rich rules over the poor, and the borrower is servant to the lender.

—Proverbs 22:7 NKJV

As a young man I had a paper route, mowed lawns, washed windows, ran errands, and did all kinds of odd jobs for people. With these various incomes I was able to open a savings account at our local bank, and was also encouraged to purchase war bonds and savings stamps at my school. Those early memories made a big impact on me and certainly helped me establish my habit of saving money.

This doesn't always mean saving in a *bank;* it can also mean saving by wise shopping.

In the beginning, saving is all give and little get. Stick with it long enough, however, and your savings will help you buy a home, educate your kids, and care for yourself in your old age. Here are a few ideas on how to become a saver.

Pay in cash. This will teach you the difference between what you want and what you really need. By paying cash, you avoid finance charges. For example, by trimming your credit card balances by $500 this year, you save $93 in interest if your card issuer charges 18.6 percent.

Make bigger down payments. When financing your next major purchase—whether a new car or a new kitchen—put up as much money as you can to reduce the principal and save interest.

If you own a home, use a home-equity loan to consolidate high-rate debts. By replacing consumer debts at 18 percent with a home-equity loan at 12 percent, you will cut your interest costs by a third. In addition, the interest on a home-equity loan can be fully deducted on your income tax return. Consolidate $10,000 in car payment and credit-card advances with a home-equity loan, and, counting the tax break, a taxpayer in the 28 percent bracket will save $936.

I want to encourage you to use great discipline in using this type of loan. The equity in your home is a very valuable asset and certainly should not be abused. You *must* stick to your plan.

Eliminate one big expense a year. Skip your winter vacation, trade in your sports car for an economy car, or discontinue your health-club membership and start using the "Y."

Take that money to pay off a loan that is costing a high interest rate, or take the same money and add to a savings or mutual fund account.

Don't pay for financial services you can get for free. Using only no-fee checking accounts, mutual funds, and credit cards can save you $100 a year or more.

Save your next raise. To squeeze out money for your 401(k), earmark your next raise for it. If you earn $40,000, a 5 percent raise will give you $2000 for your account.

Take advantage of your company savings plan. If you aren't contributing to it now, you may be throwing money away. Reason: Most 401(k)s and other plans offer tax breaks; moreover, part of your contributions are often matched by your employer.

Use your flexible spending account. Don't pass up the opportunity to pay medical and dependent-care expenses with pre-tax dollars through these accounts. A family of four is almost certain to spend $1000 a year on doctors, dentists, and prescription medicines. Your savings if you pay for them from a FSA can be at least $280.

Other savings ideas can be found right in your own home:

1. Return bottles and cans for deposit. In some states, ten a week will save $25 a year.
2. Make your own household cleaners. For an all-purpose bathroom cleaner, combine two tablespoons of either vinegar or sudsy ammonia with a quart bottle of water.

3. Think cloth rather than paper. For example, use handkerchiefs instead of facial tissues and rags instead of paper towels.

4. Place aluminum foil inside lampshades to reflect more light.

5. Clean your windows each fall to reduce your heat bill by 4 percent. Dirty glass cuts off up to 40 percent of the solar energy.

6. Don't carry junk in your car trunk. Each extra pound increases the amount of gas used.

7. Join a credit union. Not-for-profit, they usually pay more interest on deposits than banks do, and charge less interest on loans and credit cards.

8. Use disposable diapers only away from home. They cost eight times more than cloth.

9. A small vegetable garden can supply enough produce to last a family a year.

10. Put heat reflectors or foil behind radiators to heat the room, not the wall.

11. Pour flat cola in the toilet bowl. Let soak for an hour to clean.

12. Slightly overpay your mortgage each month. If you have a $100,000, 30-year mortgage at 10 percent and pay an additional $23 each month, you will pay off the loan four years earlier and save $34,344 in interest.

13. Dry heavy items in the dryer first. Next, put in lightweight ones on fluff-setting. The leftover heat will dry them.

14. Grow an aloe vera plant. When someone has a minor burn, break open a leaf and squeeze the jelly-like sap onto the injury.

15. Radial tires and adequate inflation increase car stability and cut fuel consumption by 5 to 10 percent.

Make all you can, save all you can, give all you can.
—John Wesley

Thrift, like fidelity, seems a hopelessly old-fashioned word today. Yet thrift can survive in this day of the throwaway mentality. Thrift signifies a lot more than a simple desire to save for a rainy day or a vacation to Hawaii.

Thrift is a manifestation of a whole complex of still greater virtues—moderation (my favorite word), reason, self-discipline, maturity—that together make for far more than a mere bank balance. These character words make for a strong and stable life.

Thrift is most of all a sign of *personal character*. The kind of life it yields is hard enough to fashion in the best of times, but it is much harder yet to develop in times of "I-want-it-all-right-now." We live in a society in which the undisciplined endlessly pursue the unnecessary. Getting it on easy credit is not much of a challenge. Many of us go out and buy more and more and more in order to be satisfied. We don't even have to leave our homes; we just tune into a shopping channel or browse through catalogs stuffed with the latest in high-tech gadgets.

Thrifty people save for specific goals, meaning they are less likely to buy a lot of junk in passing. They can face the tease of Madison Avenue and say, "No, thank you."

Here are some techniques dealing with banks and their services that can be helpful to your financial planning.

Banking Services

▲ If you run out of checks and stand at a merchant's cash register embarrassed, **you can write a check using your deposit slip.** Many people aren't aware of this, but your bank will accept the slip and pay. Make sure you complete it as though it were a check. Make sure you sign in the normal area of the check. In bold letters print at the bottom of the deposit slip, *"THIS IS A CHECK."*

▲ Always make it a habit to **deposit a check immediately after receiving it.** This way you minimize your risk of losing the check. A lady once came to one of my seminars and got excited about implementing my "Total Mess to Total Rest" program. The next day, while cleaning out her desk, she found a $200 check that had been in her drawer five months! (She immediately called to let me know about her find.)

▲ Ever since I was a young boy I would **put change in a jar.** When Emilie and I were dating we would do the same after each date. At the time of our wedding we had almost $400 saved in this manner. Even today I put all my quarters in a jar. This "pot of gold" has become my "mad" money for something special for myself or a birthday gift or such. Many people faithfully deposit this money in a savings account. It's amazing how this method adds to your savings account.

▲ Since you want your money working for you, **don't keep more than is necessary in a no-interest checking account.** Even in a business checking account you can float extra cash from non-interest to interest to non-interest when it's check-writing time. A few days in the interest account will contribute extra interest over a year's time.

▲ **It usually doesn't pay to postdate a check.** If your check is charged to your account before you expect it to be, it might cause other checks that you've written to bounce. This will really cause a loss of your time to straighten it out, plus the service charges add up very fast.

▲ **Put your money in a bank where interest is compounded semiannually or quarterly rather than yearly.** Your money will work harder for you.

▲ **Only in emergencies should you withdraw funds from a savings account before the stated interest payment date.**

▲ **Have your checks printed by someone other than the bank.** Two great sources for having your checks printed at a reduced price are: **"Checks in the Mail,"** P. O. Box 7802, Irwindale, CA 91706, 800-733-4443, or **"Current, Inc."** Colorado Springs, CO 80941.

▲ **Do all you can to protect your credit rating.** This is one of your most valuable assets. If for some reason you run into difficult financial times, go to your creditors *first* and tell them what's happening. If at all possible they will try to work with you.

▲ **Try to have at least two months of income in your savings account** to help during those unannounced emergencies. Six months would be better yet.

▲ **"Pay yourself a little more first"** is a great guideline when deciding to charge or pay cash. If at all possible, pay cash and put the monthly payment into your savings account. That way you get the interest rather than paying the big bad wolf. Over a period of time this will become a normal way of thinking. You can't always do this with large items, but many items can be handled this way.

▲ **Don't pay your bills before they are due.** The extra days in an interest-bearing account will give you extra interest each month.

▲ **Banks and savings and loans are not the only institutions for handling money.** If you are eligible for membership in a credit union, you should look at this alternative. Credit unions usually pay higher interest and charge less for loans and credit cards.

▲ **Shop around for the best rates on credit cards.** This is a very competitive business, and rates do vary. If you are interested in receiving a comparison listing of over 500 banks, send $5 to **RAM**, Box 1700, Frederick, MD 21702 for *CardTrak*.

▲ **If you must have a credit card, get one that will credit your dollar purchases to airplane mileage, hotel accommodations, and even merchandise.**

▲ A great idea that pays great dividends is to **buy United States saving bonds,** either through your local bank or under a payroll savings plan where you're employed. You can build up a sizable nest egg over the years by consistently purchasing a small bond.

Instead of giving another toy to an "over-toyed" grandchild, purchase a savings bond in his or her name.

▲ The key to financial success is to **spend less than is earned** and continue to do that for a lengthy period of time. Proverbs 13:11 says, "He who gathers money little by little makes it grow" (NIV).

▲ One of the basic principles of handling your money successfully is to **delay gratification.** Delayed gratification requires a long-term perspective and is the key to financial maturity. Financial maturity can be defined as "giving up today's desires for future benefits."

▲ Credit card companies estimate that **using credit cards will result in our spending 34 percent more than if we used cash.**

▲ When confronted with the opportunity to make an impulse purchase, **discipline yourself to wait at least one week before spending the money.**

▲ If you are an impulse buyer, **ask a spouse or a friend about your purchase before you give yourself the okay to purchase.** With this accountability you will find most of your impulses going away.

▲ We have some very good friends who **freeze all of their credit cards in the freezer.** Before they can charge from them they have to wait until they thaw out. In most cases they have changed their minds while they wait.

▲ If you are really serious about curtailing credit card spending, **place your credit cards (with the exception of one for emergencies) in your safe deposit box.** By the time you go to the trouble of retrieving the cards you will know if you really need the item and will have had plenty of time to think over the purchase.

Credit Is Like Gold

▲ A good way to keep out of credit binds is to **pay off a series of payments completely before committing yourself to a new series of payments for something else.** Also, be cautious of jumping into a home equity loan. For most families their equity in their home is their retirement savings. If you deplete that fund you might seriously jeopardize some of your long-term goals.

▲ If for some reason you get a bad credit rating that has an item improperly posted to your account, **be sure to correct this error immediately.** The longer it remains on your record, the harder it is to get corrected.

▲ Are you thinking about taking out a second mortgage to finance a vacation, buy an automobile, consolidate bills, or raise money to buy stocks? Although your home could be used as security for such a loan, it's probably best to take out a personal installment loan instead. **Second mortgages should not be used for casual expenditures.**

▲ **Try not to put down less than a one-third cash payment when purchasing a car,** or to let the financing extend past 36 months. With less than one-third down, a car's depreciation is likely to reduce its market value faster than you can shrink the balance of the loan.

▲ Having trouble making monthly loan payments? **Consider slicing the remaining payments in half by extending them over a longer period of time.**

▲ **Knowing and believing that God owns it all will provide total freedom from any type of financial bondage**—the bondage of either too much or too little.

PART FIVE

When You're Ready to Make Investments

▲ ▲ ▲

$ How to Save Money $
You Didn't Know You Had

If anyone does not provide for his own, and especially
for those of his household, he has denied the faith, and is
worse than an unbeliever.

—1 Timothy 5:8

Do just two or three of the suggestions listed in this chapter and the money will add up fast. In many cases you may not even be aware that these possible savings are available to you.

▲ **Give up a bad habit.** Examine your lifestyle and give up a bad habit. It might be smoking, drinking, diet drinks, candies, or cookies. You'll be amazed at the savings.

▲ **Wear tights instead of pantyhose in the winter.** The tights will save you a considerable amount over the year. They are less costly and more durable. Write for a free catalog to:

> L'eggs Brands, Inc.
> P.O. Box 748
> Rural Hill, NC 27098

▲ **Carry your own lunch.** Bring a sandwich, soft drink or juice, fruit, veggies, and a low-calorie dessert in a brown bag, and save considerably over buying lunch out. Even two or three days a week makes a big difference, and if you and your spouse both work it really makes a big savings.

▲ **Buy film and processing from a direct mail developing company.** We have used this means to purchase and process our Kodacolor film. Request information from:

> Clark Color Labs
> P.O. Box 96300
> Washington, DC 20090

They have labs all around the country and can give you the address nearest your home.

▲ **Buy a used car rather than a new one.** The amount of savings from a one- to three-year-old used car is tremendous. You can move up to a larger, more comfortable car if you are willing to buy used rather than new. If you are concerned about getting a lemon, for a few dollars you can hire a mechanic to go over the mechanics of the car to check its condition. We are talking about thousands of dollars in savings.

▲ **Make your own coffee.** Invest in an inexpensive coffee-maker, a can of coffee, and a box of dried milk. Over a year you will save almost $200 by not buying coffee each day at the snack cart or cafeteria. Bake your own muffins instead of picking one up each morning. This will be another $150 yearly.

▲ **Save something out of each paycheck.** A savings of $50 every two weeks will give you $1300 at the end of the year.

▲ **Open up a money market account.** You want your money to be drawing interest rather than just sitting in your checking account. Talk to "New Accounts" at the bank to see what programs are available.

▲ **Wash your silks.** Even though your silk blouses have "dry cleaning only" on the label, you should be able to wash them in cold water (except for prints, which might run).

▲ **Take winter clothes to a bulk dry cleaner.** You will be amazed at how much you can save by having your winter woolens cleaned by the pound rather than individually.

▲ **Don't spend your whole raise.** Take 75 percent of your next raise and put it into a savings or money market account. You might even want to take the raise money to pay off a loan that has a high interest rate. Discipline yourself not to raise your standard of living but to put yourself closer to financial freedom.

▲ **Make these changes in home heating:** Buy your fuel oil in the summertime, when prices are lower. Lower your thermostat one or more degrees (for each degree lowered you can save 3 percent of your fuel bill). Put an insulated blanket over your hot-water heater. Install a "day and night" thermostat which will give you more control when your furnace comes on and goes off.

▲ **Change light bulbs to fluorescents.** The fluorescents cost more initially but will last approximately 12 times longer and use about 25 percent less electricity.

▲ **Use the public library instead of buying books.** Depending upon your love of books, you can save several hundred dollars a year by getting a library card.

▲ **Rent a video rather than going to the movies.** Not only can a family save a lot of money on admission to the theater, but you can also save money on refreshments. You can also be preselective on what your family watches and not be caught by surprise because of violence or foul language. (Besides, popcorn made at home tastes better!)

▲ **Get an airline credit card.** I recommend this only for people who can properly use a credit card. If credit misuse is one of your weaknesses, don't get the card. If you sign up as a frequent flyer, you are frequently eligible for that airline's credit card. For every $1 you charge to the card (for all purchases), you earn one free mile of travel. This could save you a lot of money on that round-trip air ticket next summer.

▲ **Air conditioners don't have to refrigerate a room.** It isn't cost-effective to operate your air conditioner below 70°. If your outside temperature cools down in the evening, open a window or door to cool down the whole house. As with the furnace, you can save a lot of money on energy by installing a "day and night" thermostat. Turn the system off while you're away at work and set it to come on an hour before you arrive home so you have a cool home when you arrive. (No use cooling the house when you aren't home!)

▲ **Cook at home, don't eat out.** Our kitchens have sold out to the fast food industry. We have forgotten how to cook. Get some new recipes and take a cooking class, but stop going to hamburger havens for the next meal. Not only will this practice be cheaper, but the family will like it better and it will provide more nutritional value. Save going out for that special treat and occasion.

▲ **Use coupons at the grocery store.** Look in your magazines, newspapers, or throwaway inserts for coupons which will save you $.25 to $.50 on your next purchase. Some stores even offer "double redemption" on certain days. (See Chapter 46 on couponing.)

$ Why Save? $

In America we must develop the habit and good discipline of saving. Unfortunately, since World War II we have based our economy on *consumerism*—spend, spend, spend.

Here are some excellent reasons for saving.

▲ **Accumulating money so it can be put to work.** If you don't save, you will have no money for investing and lending.

▲ **Building a retirement fund.** You must have more than Social Security in your old age. It was originally intended to be only a supplement to other retirement funds.

▲ **Having money for difficult times.** You should have at least two to six months' salary set aside for emergencies.

▲ **Having money for pleasure.** All work and no play makes Johnny very boring. With good money management there must be time for fun, like a vacation, a new dress, a new suit, a second car, a boat for the lake, and to accumulate funds to invest in the stock market. You can make your own fun list!

An ideal savings goal is 10 percent of your after-tax income each year. There will be seasons in your family's life when you may not be able to meet this goal, but save *something* each month anyway.

You need to be very committed to save or you will never get started. Here are several strategies that can help you.

141

Savings from taxes. Many families overpay their taxes by having an inaccurate W4 form filled out with their employer. Adjust this form so you don't overpay. If you have been getting a refund each year of $800, by making a single adjustment you can have an extra $66.67 each month in take-home pay.

Sign up for your company's bond-a-month plan or stock option program. Use this $66.67 per month to invest in your company's investment programs.

Saving after paying off a loan. When you finish making that last payment on a car, a boat, or furniture, rather than going into more debt, keep sending the bank a check for the same amount, only this time, instead of a loan coupon, enclose a savings deposit slip. Since you have been getting by without this money for several months, continue doing without it, but this time save it.

Freeing up money to save. Here are three ways to reduce your expenses, which could free up hundreds of dollars per year.

1. **Check your life insurance.** Switch your whole life or straight life policy to a term policy. This is a very good idea while you are young. As you get older, term insurance rates become expensive, but by that time your money needs are less.

2. **Check your auto insurance.** Review with your agents to see where you can reduce premiums. Look at the special discount offerings: safe driver, senior citizen, multiple cars, low-mileage rates, etc. Even having your homeowner policy with the same carrier may give you reduced rates.

3. **Check your homeowner's or tenant's insurance.** Make sure your deduction is no less than $500. You really don't want to file a claim less than that. It will be a negative on your record and cause an increase or possible cancellation on your policy.

Real savings begin when you have the right reason to save. Once you get in the habit of saving, it becomes fun. Even small amounts on a regular basis can be exciting.

▲ Save your small change in a big coin bank. When full, deposit the money in your savings account.

▲ Bank a raise or at least part of it.

▲ Bank any Christmas bonus.

▲ Bank any unexpected income, such as bonuses, tax refunds, profits, or inheritances.

Seven Ways to Get Greater Mutual Fund Returns [1]

$ $

> *How much better is wisdom than gold, and understanding than silver!*
>
> —Proverbs 16:16 TLB

Years ago relatively little was known about mutual funds by most people. The majority of investments were made by individuals buying individual company stock. Today's trend is that individuals are going with the professional mutual funds. Unless you have the time and resources to thoroughly research your own investment portfolio, you would be advised to invest in a reputable mutual fund.

Before you purchase any mutual fund, consider these seven areas of concern:

1. Total performance that really works for you. Don't look only at yield or capital appreciation. Factor in both figures, and then subtract the load fee, the management fee, the 12b-1 fee, and any other hidden costs of owning the fund.

2. Professional management with a proven track record. Consider the track record of the fund manager over the past three years, and the track record of the fund family. Some fund families (such as Vanguard) have a knack of doing most things very well. It's no coincidence that their funds also perform well.

3. Fund switching made easy. Markets change, and you want to be able to change funds easily and without penalty. The fund should have free or reasonable ($5) switching fees and an 800 number that isn't busy during heavy trading days. Make sure the fund has no back-end load, liquidation fee, or redemption fee.

4. Rewards that outweigh risks. Generally, mutual funds spread your risk by investing in many stocks, with professional management to check out the dangers. Not all funds promise safety, however. If you're conservative, don't buy aggressive growth funds; if you're trying to reduce taxes, steer away from funds with turnover rates above 100 percent.

5. No "dividend loads" hidden in fund. Some mutual fund families invent new ways of charging you hidden loads. One sneaky way of charging investors a sales loan is to levy a fee, up to 7.25 percent, for reinvesting dividends. If your statement says "reinvesting dividend at the offering rather than the net asset value," or "at offer," take your dividends in cash and invest them elsewhere.

6. Dividend distribution dates. Reduce your tax liability by always buying *after*, never before, dividends are distributed. Ask what dates the fund distributes its dividends. Growth funds in particular usually distribute the last month of every year. Some funds pay dividends every six months, some quarterly, some even monthly.

7. Customer service that works for you. The fund families for which I've found the best customer service are: Vanguard, Financial/Invesco, and T. Rowe Price. Polite, attentive, responsive customer service really makes a difference. Many fund families also offer a variety of service, such as free telephone switching, free dividend reinvestment plans, even IRA management.

$ Investing with the $
Long-Term in Mind

Never be lazy in your work, but serve the Lord enthusiastically.

—Romans 12:11 TLB

As Americans we have lost the virtue of looking at life through long-distance lenses. We want results *now*; make it fast and profitable! In the first sections of this book we have encouraged the "little-by-little" idea of accumulating your wealth.

Those who take the long view reap the rewards of significant long-term advantages.

▲ The long view tends to smooth out the short-term fluctuations and cycles of the financial markets. Long-term investors profit from long-term trends, which have always been positive for stocks, bonds, real estate, and many other investments.

▲ Continuous and periodic investing over the long term helps reduce much of the risk associated with investing. Techniques such as "dollar-cost averaging" (investing fixed dollar amounts at periodic intervals, regardless of fluctuations in price) help investors exercise the discipline required by long-term investing.

▲ For those investments that pay interest or dividends now or in the future, the positive effects of compounding escalate with time. As interest and dividends are reinvested, they generate more and more income at an ever-increasing rate.

▲ Long-term investments can help alleviate the eroding effects of inflation when the combination of capital gains and income grow at a rate that exceeds the rate of inflation.

▲ The psychological benefits of long-term investing are substantial. Investors with the long view are not panicked by short-term declines, nor are they overly zealous about sudden gains. Instead, they place these events in their proper perspective.

$ Principles of $ Long-Term Investing

T here are nine basic principles you need to consider when making long-term investments.[1]

Principle 1:
Write Out Clear and Specific Goals

When you write down on paper what your plans are, you are more likely to put these goals into action. Ask yourself, "What am I trying to accomplish with my money?"

▲ Do I want the principal to grow over time?

▲ Do I need to reduce my tax obligations?

▲ Do I need to plan for retirement?

▲ Do I need to provide for my children's education?

The answers to such questions will help give direction to your specific investment goals.

Your second major question should be, "What is my tolerance for risk?" Are you able to live with your investment taking downturns because of market influence, variations in interest rates, changes in the economy, political changes, and changes in the tax laws?

Are you willing to assume the risks associated with an aggressive strategy that may reap significant rewards, or are you more comfortable with a conservative approach that emphasizes safety?

When you know the answer to these questions, you can begin to select the long-term investments that are most likely to meet your goals.

Principle 2: Research
Your Investment Before You Invest

Long-term investing requires patience and discipline. Patience means that such investing is a long-term process. Discipline is commitment to the long-term view. The people around you will likely be short-term, thereby causing you stress because of the difference in the two ideas.

You must make investment decisions only after careful investigation, whether of stocks, bonds, insurance, or real estate. To judge value takes time. Investigate before you invest.

Principle 3: Make Sure You
Understand the Difference Between
Investment and Trading

Investing is when you hold an investment over a long period of time. When you buy an investment product for a short period of time and then sell it for a short-term profit or loss, you are *trading*.

Trading and investing are different things and require different strategies. Trading for short-term gains is a valid strategy for those who are willing to accept the risks and understand that it is not investing.

Principle 4:
Maintain Future Orientation

The true investor is future-looking and can live with daily and seasonal swings and cycles of the financial markets. Despite short-term fluctuations, the long-term trend has always been a positive one for stocks, bonds, real estate, and other investments.

Over the last 60 years the total return of the stock market has averaged about 10 percent per year compounded annually. This compares to 3 percent inflation per year over the same period. When viewed in proper perspective, short-term fluctuations are just squiggles on a long-term line.

Principle 5:
Review Your Investments Regularly

You must review your goals and investments regularly. At least once a month we analyze both of these to see if we are on target. If not, we make the necessary changes to maximize our long-term financial direction. Just because your investments are long-term doesn't mean you buy them and store them in a safe deposit box. Financial markets and world economics may fundamentally change, so you need to make changes in your portfolio when the markets change.

Principle 6: Take Advantage of Worldwide Opportunities

As a young man I was able to distinguish the various different markets in the world. There were specific boundaries where the American market started and stopped. But the global economics of the 1990s isn't that clear. What happens in Japan and Germany is often related to what's going on in America. Before you venture out into new waters, make sure you do a thorough job in researching the new market.

Principle 7: Make Sure Your Investment for the Long-Term Represents Quality

Your initial investigation must consider the organization's reputation for quality. As we know by reading many of the new business books which stress excellence, the underlying principle of business success is *quality*. Quality is not an art but a science; it doesn't just happen randomly, but must be planned for. You want companies that put high value on the future. They are willing to spend large sums of money in research and resources for the long term.

Investments with a reputation for quality will have a higher value over the long run than those that don't.

Principle 8: Use the Safety Benefits of Being a Long-Term Investor

When the total rate of return is a combination of interest or dividend yield plus capital gains, and the combination of these is greater than inflation, then we have been able to hedge against inflation—one of our long-term goals.

Principle 9: Appreciate Your Investment When Its Money Is Able to Earn Money

Many investors fail to recognize the true worth of certain investments—those in which interest and/or dividends earned are compounded over time. This is especially true if income accrues on a tax-free or tax-deferred basis.

As your principal earns interest or dividends, that new money may also earn income if you reinvest it. In effect, your income earns additional income.

As long as you continue to reinvest interest and dividends, the cycle will repeat itself throughout the life of the investment.

The Rule of 72 is a mathematical formula that dramatically illustrates the long-range time value of compounding interest and dividends. To approximate the time it will take for a given amount of money to double at a specific compound interest rate, simply divide 72 by the interest rate. For example, the long-term average compounded returned, with dividends reinvested, for common stocks was about 10 percent per year for the period between 1926 and 1987. Therefore, at a compound annual rate of 10 percent, $1000 would have grown to $2000 in about 7.2 years (72 divided by 10 equals 7.2).

Here are several long-term investments that you might want to consider for your portfolio:

Growth Investments

▲ Common stocks
▲ Direct investments in a project
▲ Partnerships in a project or group of projects

Fixed-Income Investments

▲ Long-term Treasury bonds
▲ Municipal bonds
▲ Mortgage-backed securities
▲ Corporate bonds

Growth-and-Income Investments

▲ Mutual funds
▲ Unit investment trusts
▲ Insurance and annuities
▲ Real estate

$ Consider a Discount Broker $

When it comes time for you to expand your money management beyond your local bank and its interest-earning accounts, you will want to consider investments in stocks and bonds. When you do, you will need to consider what services you want this company to perform for you.

If you are new in this area of investments, you might want to interview various sales representatives from nationally known brokerage firms. They will use their research analysts to provide you with stock recommendations on particular companies.

This type of firm can be of great assistance, but the services will cost you more than you might be willing to pay. Also, you may not need or want all of these services. You may only need someone to help you purchase stocks and bonds for your portfolio. In that case you want to choose a qualified discount brokerage firm.

The difference in fees between these two types of firms can be significant. According to a recent survey, a full-service broker will charge an average of $218 for a particular type of transaction and a discount broker will charge an average of $56. You might be asking, "Why the big difference?" The answer is *advice*.

Full-service brokerage houses usually provide their customers with investment reports containing buy and sell recommendations. You are paying for this service.

Discount brokers won't give you any advice on what to buy or sell. They merely execute trades at the customer's request. You can usually get printout copies of Value Line and Standard & Poor's research reports, but the discount brokers give no personalized advice.

Your decision on which type of broker to use is based on whether you need advice. You should also consider whether the full-service broker can provide some other valuable service that is worth the cost difference.

If you answer no to these two questions, you should strongly consider a discount broker, since the cost savings are considerable. The bigger the trade, the bigger the difference in price. The big discounters do not always have the lowest rates, but they do have more products to sell. In addition to stocks, they also sell bonds and mutual funds. Shopping around can be worth your effort.

You might ask, "Where do I find a discount broker?" Referrals from friends are sometimes the best. You can also check the yellow pages in your phone book or the 1992 survey published by Mercer, Inc. of New York. You can buy this discount brokerage directory for less than $40 by calling 800-582-9854. (This directory is a two-volume edition, and you need both volumes.)

Other sources to consider:

▲ **The Discount Investing Directory**, Phillips Publishing Inc., 7811 Montrose Road, Potomac, MD 20854, 800-777-5005.

▲ **Barry Murphy & Co.**, 270 Congress St., Boston, MA 02210, 800-288-1400, 617-426-1770.

▲ **Brown & Co.**, 20 Winthrop Square, Boston, MA 02110, 800-225-6707, 617-742-2600.

▲ **Jack White & Co.**, 9191 Towne Centre Dr., Suite 220, San Diego, CA 92122, 800-233-3411, 619-587-2000.

▲ **Marquette de Bary Co.**, 488 Madison Ave., New York, NY 10022, 800-221-3305, 212-644-5300.

▲ **Pacific Brokerage Services**, 5757 Wilshire Blvd., Suite 3, Los Angeles, CA 90036, 800-421-8395, 213-939-1100.

Your money is not at more risk with a discount broker. Your funds are just as fully protected, regulated, and insured—to at least $500,000—as with a full-price broker. Perhaps the name "discount" may be misleading. Discount brokers are not selling inferior goods for less money. They sell the same stock certificates, use the same clearinghouses, and endure the same strict SEC rules as the big boys.

Compound Interest: The Eighth Wonder of the World

He who gathers money little by little makes it grow.
—Proverbs 13:11 NIV

As I have shared with you in an earlier chapter, one of my friends often refers to compound interest as "the eighth wonder of the world." Two basic principles—

▲ **Earn** little by little
▲ **Save** little by little

—will help you start on the road to financial freedom.

If you can accumulate $10,000 in a savings account in the next four years and then let it grow at an 8 percent interest rate without any further additions for the next 40 years, it will be worth $217,245 (or $930,510 at a 12 percent growth rate, $3.8 million at 16 percent, and $5.3 million at 17 percent).

Look at the same situation another way. Assume that you put $2000 away into an untouchable account at the end of each year. At the end of 40 years you would have $518,113 at an 8 percent return, $1.5 million at 12 percent, $4.7 million at 16 percent, and $6.3 million at 17 percent.

Two lessons here: first, *the importance of sacrificing early in your career* to start accumulating a capital base. The time value of money is incredibly important.

154

Second, *the rate of return is important.* The difference of just 1 percent in the above examples (between 16 and 17 percent return) becomes substantial in the long term.

Of course, these examples assume no annual tax on earnings, so the money would have to be invested in a tax-free instrument such as an IRA, an annuity plan, or municipal bonds. You can talk to your bank or financial adviser on specific recommendations.[1]

Grow Through Reinvesting Your Dividends

Much is required from those to who much is given, for their responsibility is greater.

—Luke 12:48 TLB

Can you delay your gratification? If you can patiently wait for future fulfillment you should consider reinvesting your investment dividends as a strategy to see your wealth grow. You might ask, "Why reinvest dividends?" Because the stock market has superior wealth-building power. Few other investment tools can multiply your wealth like the stock market. In the years since 1926, a single $1000 investment in money markets or bonds would have grown to between $10,000 and $20,000 (depending upon which bond you owned). But an investment in stocks, with dividends reinvested, would today be worth $535,000—over 25 times the value of buy-and-hold bonds or cash. Nearly half of these gains would have come from reinvested dividends alone.

You can enjoy this kind of gain by purchasing stocks that historically pay regular and rising dividends. By contributing a small amount of added money on a regular basis and by reinvesting the quarterly dividends into the purchase of additional stock, you can see your investment dollars grow rapidly.

By investing with companies that have a Dividend Reinvestment Plan (DRIP), you can save broker fees and commissions by going directly to the company to purchase their stock. In fact, some of the companies will even give you a 5 percent discount for reinvesting dividends or buying more shares.

If you don't presently own shares in these companies, you will need to buy one or more shares from your broker, and then you can contact the company directly. Either way, this proven method locks in superb gains from your core blue-chip stock and utilities holdings. Since dividends are usually paid quarterly, this is a great way to boost your number of shares every three months. You can also add new shares on a regular basis by investing a fixed number of dollars each month or quarter (called "dollar-cost averaging"). See the next chapter to learn about this strategy.

This plan should only be *part* of your investment strategy; it is not designed for an entire well-balanced portfolio. However, this portion of investment dollars will give you a good investment return.

Each company that offers a DRIP has a special shareholder-relations office which takes care of dividend reinvestments and new stock purchases free of commissions. Certain guidelines apply, such as minimum initial investment levels and maximum monthly or quarterly amounts.

How to Get Started

You may already own blue chip or utility stock that has a DRIP plan. If you do, you can contact the special shareholder office and request information on reinvesting. The prospectus will outline the company's requirements. Each company is different, so read the information carefully.

If you are a new investor, the best place to start is with a company that offers you *total* commission-free investing from the very first share. By simply buying one share (or more) directly from the company, you can reinvest dividends and buy as many more shares as you want *totally* free of charge. Two of my recommended stocks offer such a program:

▲ **Proctor & Gamble**, C/O P&G Shareholders Services, 2 Proctor & Gamble Plaza, Cincinnati, OH 45202-3314, 800-742-6523 or 513-983-1100. Minimum: one share (about $85).

▲ **Texaco**, 2000 Westchester Ave., White Plains, NY 10650, 914-253-6072. Minimum: $250 to start.

With these two stocks you never need to use a broker. Buy all your P&G or Texaco shares (just $2 per fractional share for P&G) directly from the company.

DRIP Plans with 5 Percent Discounts

Some companies not only let you buy shares commission-free, but they give you a discount on your purchase!

This is one strategy that can multiply your money as rapidly as any I know of, and these high-dividend (7 to 9 percent) utilities offer better-than-money-market income, with a good chance for long-term capital gains as well. By investing in a DRIP plan with these companies, vou're making money in three ways at once: high income, long-term capital gains, and zero "friction" costs from commissions.

Here are seven companies which offer discounts on shares purchased with reinvested dividends *and* which offer high dividends:

Central Maine Power Co. .... 5% discount	NUI Corp. .... 5% discount
E'Town Corp. 5%	Public Service Co. of Colorado 3%
Health Care REIT Inc. 4%	Texas Utilities Co. . 5%
New Plan Realty Trust 5%	

E'Town Corp. (OTC: EWAT; formerly Elizabethtown Water Co.) and Health Care REIT Inc. (NYSE: HCP) also let enrollees in their dividend reinvestment plans use optional cash purchases to purchase new stock at a discount to the market price (5 percent for E'Town and 4 percent for Health Care REIT).

E'Town's 5 percent discount means you could spend just $25.65 to buy a share selling on the open market for $27. Plus you save on commissions! Remember, you must buy at least 20 shares from your broker before qualifying for the E'Town plan.

Here is a condensed list of companies offering a dividend reinvestment plan.

Blue Chip Stocks

Allied Signal
(NYSE: ALD)
P.O. Box 50000R
Morristown, NJ 07960
210-455-2127
Current yield: 2.0%
Approx. share price: 50

Bristol-Myers Squibb
(NYSE: BMY)
345 Park Avenue
New York, NY 10154
($10-2500/month)
Current yield: 3.1%
Approx. share price: 80

Chevron
(NYSE: CHV)
225 Bush Street
San Francisco, CA 94104
415-894-7700
Current yield: 4.9%
Approx. share price: 65

Du Pont
(NYSE: DD)
1007 Market Street
Wilmington, DE 19898
302-774-9656
($10-1000/quarter)
Current yield: 3.8%
Approx. share price: 47

Exxon
(NYSE: XON)
225 E. John W. Carpenter Fwy.
Irving, TX 75062
214-444-1900
($10-60,000/year)
Current yield: 4.9%

Exxon (cont'd)
Approx. share price: 55

General Mills
(NYSE: GIS)
P.O. Box 1113
Minneapolis, MN 55440
612-540-3888
($10-3000/quarter)
Current yield: 2.3%
Approx. share price: 65

IBM
(NYSE: IBM)
C/O First Chicago Trust Co.-NY
P.O. Box 7896
Church Street Station
New York, NY 10249
212-735-7000
($10-5000/quarter)
Current yield: 5.8%
Approx. sales price: 82

Lilly (Eli) & Co.
(NYSE: LLY)
Lilly Corporate Center
Indianapolis, IN 46285
800-833-8699
($25-25,000/year)
Current yield: 3.1%
Approx. share price: 71

Mobil Corp.
(NYSE: MOB)
150 E. 42nd Street
New York, NY 10017-5666
800-648-9291
($10-5000/month)
Current yield: 5.4%
Approx. share price: 60

Philip Morris
(NYSE: MO)
212-880-5000
($10-60,000/year)
Current yield: 2.8%
Approx. share price: 75

Procter & Gamble
(NYSE: PG)
C/O Shareholder Services
2 Procter & Gamble Plaza
Cincinnati, OH 45202-3314
800-742-6253 or
800-582-2685 (in Ohio) or
513-983-1100
Current yield: 2.5%
Approx. share price: 52

Raytheon
(NYSE: RTN)
141 Spring Street
Lexington, MA 02173
617-862-6600
($10-5000/quarter)
Current yield: 2.9%
Approx. share price: 89

Utilities

* **Central Maine Power Co**.
(NYSE: CTP)
Edison Drive
Augusta, ME 04336
800-695-4267
($10-30,000/year)
Current yield: 7.7%
Approx. share price: 20

DPL Inc.
(NYSE: DPL)
P.O. Box 1247
Dayton, OH 45401
415-259-7150
($25-1000/quarter)
Current yield: 6.6%
Approx. share price: 25

† **E'Town Corp**.
(NASDAQ: EWAT)
P.O. Box 788
600 South Avenue
Westfield, NJ 07091-0788

E'Town Corp. (cont'd)
908-654-1234
Current yield: 7.4%
Approx. share price: 28

New England Electric
(NYSE: NES)
P.O. Box 770
Westborough, MA 01581-0770
508-366-9011
Current yield: 6.6%
Approx. share price: 30

Northwestern Public Service Co.
(NYSE: NPS)
3rd Street & Dakota Ave. So.
Huron, SD 57350
605-352-8411, ext. 403
($10-5000/quarter)
Current yield: 6.1%
Approx. share price: 27

* **NUI Corp.**
(NYSE: NUI)
550 Rte. 202/206, Box 760
Bedminster, NJ 07921-0760
201-781-0500
($25-3000/quarter)
Current yield: 8.5%
Approx. share price: 21

* **Public Service Co. of Colorado**
(NYSE: PSR)
P.O. Box 840, Room 160B
Denver, CO 80201-0840
303-571-7514
($25-100,000/year)
Current yield: 7.7%
Approx. share price: 26

* **Texas Utilities Co.**
201 Bryan Tower
Dallas, TX 75201
214-812-4646

Texas Utilities Co. (cont'd)
($25-3000/quarter)
Current yield: 7.4%
Approx. share price: 37

Union Electric
(NYSE: UEP)
P.O. Box 149
St. Louis, MO 63166
800-255-2237
(0-$60,000/year)
Current yield: 6.8%
Approx. share price: 33

WPL Holdings
(NYSE: WPH)
P.O. Box 2568
Madison, WI 53701-2568
800-356-5343
($20-3000/month)
Current yield: 6.0%
Approx. share price: 31

REITS

* **Health Care REIT Inc.**
(NYSE: HCP)
1 Seagate, Ste. 1950
Toledo, OH 43604
419-247-2800
($10-2500/quarter)
Current yield: 9.1%
Approx. share price: 20

† **New Plan Realty Trust**
(NYSE: NPR)
1120 Avenue of the Americas
New York, NY 10036
212-869-3000

New Plan Realty (cont'd)
($100-5000/quarter)
Current yield: 5.9%
Approx. share price: 20

Weingartner Realty Investors
(NYSE: WRI)
C/O Ameritrust Co.
P.O. Box 6477
Cleveland, OH 44101
216-737-5742
($100-15,000/semiannually)
Current yield: 6.5%
Approx. share price: 31

Remember, every investment involves some degree of risk, so investigate any stock carefully before buying.

---

*Offers discount on reinvested dividends.

†Offers discounts on reinvested dividends *and* optional cash purchases.

$ Dollar-Cost $
Averaging

There is an old rule in buying stock which says "Buy low and sell high." That is a truism, but most of us aren't smart enough to know where the low is and where the high might be. To help you in this matter, you can smooth out market fluctuations and make more money in the long run by dollar-cost averaging your investments in stocks, whether from a regular stockbroker, a discount stockbroker, or a company offering a DRIP (Dividend Reinvestment Plan).

Set aside a certain dollar figure per month or quarter. With DRIPS, this can be as little as $10 a month or quarter. When the price of a stock or fund is down, you automatically buy more shares (or fractions of a share), and when the price is higher, your fixed contribution buys fewer shares.

For example, let's say you invest $100 per quarter in a stock. If it is selling at $10 per share today, your $100 buys 10 shares. Then let's say the market drops to $5 per share. In that case your next quarterly payment buys 20 shares. The following quarter the share price soars to $20. That means your $100 buys only five shares. Then the market returns to normal and your stock returns to $10 per share, and you buy 10 shares with your final $100 contribution.

Let's add it all up: In the course of one year you've invested $400 and bought a total of 45 shares, for an average price of $8.89 per share. Yet the average price for the year was $11.25 ($45 divided by 4). So you managed to save 21 percent per share, and you never had to outguess the market.

With most DRIP plans, you can set aside as little as $5 or $10 per month and pay no commissions.

No system is foolproof, so that you can relax and not give any thought to your investments. There is no such thing as an ideal long-term investment. Most stocks go in and out of favor with investors, and some reach their maximum efficiency as a producer of goods or services. You have to be aware of what your companies do and what their continuing potential for growth and increased earnings might be.

Market timing is crucial: The '80s were hot on computer stocks, but the '90s seem to favor biotech offerings. Every decade has one or more best type of investment.

That is why "Blue Chip" stocks are so popular; they seem to endure time and cycles of the market. Even with the "Blue Chippers," though, you have to stay awake at the wheel.

$ Real Estate Profits $
Can Be Reduced

Emilie and I live in California. Here real estate purchases have been a great way to increase wealth or to build a sizable nest egg for retirement. There are incredible stories of people buying homes in the '60s for $35,000, putting in normal improvements, and 25 years later selling them for over $600,000.

That's a great story if you don't have to pay the capital gains taxes! Even with the following ideas, people who live in certain desirable states will pay a large tax when they sell. However, in most of the 50 states these ideas will certainly help reduce your profit taxes.

Take a $125,000 Tax Exemption
When You Sell Your Home

Special rules apply to the sale of a principal home by persons age 55 or older. If either you or your spouse were age 55 or older on the date of the sale, and 1) you owned and lived in the house for at least three of the past five years, and 2) you or your spouse have not used the exemption before, then you may elect to completely exclude up to $125,000 of the profit from taxable income regardless of whether you buy another home. You may only use the age 55 exclusion *one time*, regardless of how much profit you realize.

If your spouse has already taken the exclusion, even if it was prior to your marriage, neither of you can claim another exclusion unless the original exclusion was revoked within three years. Within two years of selling your home, if you purchase and live in another home that costs at least as much as the adjusted sales price of the old home, your entire gain on the sale is not taxed. In that case, you should save your $125,000 exclusion and use it when you sell your second home.

But if you sell your home and purchase another home for an amount *less* than the home you sold, you might be better off taking the $125,000 exclusion now. See IRS Publication 523, "Tax Information on Selling Your Home."

Sell Your Home, Remain There, and Take a Tax Deduction Too

If you are over 55 and no longer want the problems of home ownership, you can sell your home, take the onetime tax exemption of $125,000 on the home sale, and still *stay in your house*. Here's how.

Sell your home to an investor (perhaps one of your adult children). The investor then leases the home back to you, perhaps for the remainder of your life. You'll avoid the headaches of dealing with rising property taxes, difficult upkeep, higher insurance, and major repairs. The buyer will get monthly rental income from you, plus the buyer can take advantage of tax depreciation credits and other write-offs.

Of course, you must pay a fair market rent, or else the IRS will disallow any rental deductions the buyer takes.

Make a Tax-Free Swap of Your Property

One very handy provision of the tax law allows you to use the increase in value of an old property to help you buy a new one—without paying any tax on the increase. The rule is called a "tax-free swap," and the only restriction is that both the old and the new properties must be "like kind properties"; that is, they must be the same type of property.

Tax reducer tip: Swap your small house in an overpriced city for a bigger house in a less-expensive place. Or swap a rental property in one resort area for another rental property in a different area. Just be sure that the new properties are at least as expensive and the same kind as the old ones.

Use Your Home Equity as a Tax Shelter

Interest paid on home equity lines of credit secured by a house or vacation home is fully tax-deductible up to $100,000 annually. So one of your best bets as a tax shelter—and one of the few remaining tax shelters at all—is the home equity loan. And now a new law helps you decide what loan terms you should choose. The law will require the lender to provide:

▲ Complete information about interest rates and costs when giving you a loan application.

▲ Honest ads about home equity loans.

▲ Dependable loan terms, with no unilateral changes in due dates.

Real estate is still one of the best investments a person or couple can make. The American dream is to own a home, although each year it becomes more and more difficult for the first-time buyer to make that dream come true. None of us knows what the future of real estate will be, but with increasing population in our country, the principle of supply and demand states that desirable property will have equity-building capabilities.

Make sure that your first home fits into your ability to make the monthly payments without placing undue strain on your long-term budget. Over a long period of time, larger mortgage payments than you can reasonably make become regressive, not progressive. The extra stress will have a negative effect on your life.

House Rich, Cash Poor

Do not fear, for I am with you; do not be dismayed, for I am your God. I will strengthen you and help you; I will uphold you with my righteous right hand.

—Isaiah 41:10 NIV

As our country becomes a graying society, we will find more and more home-owners over 62 years of age who have paid off their home mortgages but now have minimal income. What do you do when you are house rich but cash poor? In August of 1989, the Federal Housing Administration entered into a pilot program with 25,000 loans available to help correct this situation.

The concept was developed to help older people from being forced to leave their homes at any future date.

This program is commonly referred to as a "reverse mortgage" and is designed to help elderly homeowners cash in on their equity. Here is how a reverse mortgage works.

▲ It is available to any homeowner who is at least 62 years of age and whose house or condo is completely paid for or is substantially debt-free.

▲ There is no minimum loan amount. The maximum loan amount is based on a percentage of your home's value and on a limit that varies from area to area.

- ▲ Homeowners have a choice: They can receive monthly payments, a line of credit, or a single lump sum. The older you are and the more valuable the home, the larger your monthly payments.

- ▲ The payments do not affect Social Security or Medicare benefits.

- ▲ The mortgages do not allow a lender to force you to sell or vacate your home if the money owed on the loan exceeds the value of the home. FHA insurance will cover any balance due the lender.

- ▲ The mortgages do not require repayment until you die, sell, or move out of your home.

If you are a senior citizen, or if you have parents who are in this situation, you can obtain additional information about this program by contacting your local HUD or FHA offices. Check the yellow pages for telephone numbers.

$ Should You Refinance $
Your Mortgage?

During the early '90s we saw interest rates plummet much lower than we ever thought possible. When interest rates go down this much, people ask, "Should I refinance my mortgage?" This chapter will help with that crucial decision.

Refinancing your mortgage is simply taking out a new mortgage on your home.

Typically, refinancing a mortgage requires the same procedures and costs associated with purchasing a new home: application fees, origination fees, and closing costs which are paid by the borrower.

In some situations, refinancing your mortgage may be a sound credit decision. Falling interest rates can be such a situation. Other factors need to be considered, however, before you trade in your old mortgage for a new one. To help you decide, consider these objectives in refinancing:

▲ **Reduce monthly mortgage payments.** By replacing your high-interest-rate mortgage with one at a lower rate, you will reduce your monthly payment.

▲ **Obtain cash by accessing the equity in your home.** For example, if you pay off a $100,000 mortgage balance and replace it with a $150,000 mortgage, you'll have $50,000 for home improvements, a college education, or a major purchase.

▲ **Take advantage of tax deductions on mortgage interest expense.** Those who own their own homes free and clear, or who have a small mortgage balance remaining, may consider refinancing to gain tax deductibility on the interest expense. According to the Revenue Act of 1987, up to $100,000 of refinanced debt, plus the amount of your existing mortgage, is eligible for tax deductibility.

When is it worthwhile to refinance your existing mortgage at a lower rate?

As a general rule, refinancing is worthwhile when your current mortgage rate is at least 2 percent higher than prevailing market interest rates. This 2 percent figure is a cost-effective margin when weighing the costs of refinancing against the savings in monthly payments.

Another consideration is how long you plan to own your home. For example, if you have a $150,000 mortgage, you would need to remain in your home for at least two years before the savings in your monthly payment recoups the cost of refinancing. The chart below can help you estimate how long it would take to realize the savings of a refinancing.

REFINANCE RECOVERY CHART

Current monthly mortgage payment $_____

Minus monthly payment at new rate   −$_____
    (See payment table below)

Monthly savings at new rate   =$_____
                      × 12

Yearly savings at new rate   =$_____
                                      (A)

Refinancing Costs† $_____
                                        (B)

Years to recover the costs of refinancing (B divided by A)   _____

---

† Includes closing costs, application fee, origination points (approximately 2%-4% of loan amount, depending on loan size).

PAYMENT TABLE

Equal Monthly Payments to Amortize a Loan of $1000

Term Rate (%)	15 Years	25 Years	30 Years
7	8.99	7.07	6.65
7½	9.27	7.39	6.99
8	9.56	7.72	7.34
8½	9.85	8.05	7.69
9	10.14	8.39	8.05
9½	10.44	8.74	8.41
10	10.75	9.09	8.78
10½	11.05	9.44	9.15
11	11.37	9.80	9.52
11½	11.68	10.16	9.90
12	12.00	10.53	10.29

To calculate your monthly payments:

$$\frac{\text{Loan amount}}{1000} \quad X \quad \text{Payment factor from chart above}$$

For example, the monthly payment on a $100,000, 15-year mortgage at an interest rate of 10½ percent would be calculated as follows:

$$\frac{\$100,000}{1000} \quad X \quad 11.05 \quad = \quad \$1105 \text{ per month}$$

You may want to consult your tax adviser for advice and tax implications on this decision.

PART SIX

Your Children's Money Management

▲ ▲ ▲

Children Learn Money Habits Early

Train up a child in the way he should go, and even when he is old he will not depart from it.

—Proverbs 22:6

We live in a world where adults find themselves in financial woes. How do people learn about money? Usually by trial and error. Few families take the time to teach their children how to be smart with money.

Children who learn about money at an early age will be ahead of the game. As early as preschool a child can be given a piggy bank and taught about coins. You will want to teach your child that you don't save money the same way you collect pinecones. You save it because it is a medium of exchange for other things you want—for yourself and others.

Learning to deal with money properly will foster discipline, good work habits, and self-respect in your children. Here are several ways you can help your children get a good handle on money.

Start with an Allowance

An allowance usually begins in grade school. Most experts advise not to tie an allowance directly to a child's daily chores. Children should help around the home not because they get paid for it, but because they share responsibilities as members of a family. However, you might pay a child for doing extra jobs at home. This can develop his or her initiative. We know of parents who give stickers to their children when they aren't asked to do something but do it anyway. At the child's discretion the stickers can be redeemed for 25 cents each. This has been a great motivator for building initiative and teamwork in the family.

How large should the allowance be? This depends on your individual status. It should be based on a fair budget that allows for entertainment, snacks, lunch money, bus fare, and school supplies. Add some extra money to include money for the church and for savings. Rather than arbitrarily setting the amount, talk with your child about your expectations of what the money should be used for, and then decide together what a good amount would be.

Start at $2 a week and work up to $3 by the fifth grade. A child younger than ten shouldn't get more than $5. If you give an eight-year-old $5, what will he expect when he's 12?

Give the allowance semimonthly by age seven or eight because this grants more responsibility and decision-making power. The best thing that could happen is for your child to spend the money all at once and then have to go two weeks without any money or be forced to take money out of his or her savings. (Most kids hate to do this. By age eight they become very protective of their savings.)

By age 12 all children need to be getting an allowance. This is a good way to give independence in a nondangerous way to the preteen, who is struggling for self-reliance anyway.

Although you can have input into how your child spends his money, you shouldn't cut back or eliminate the allowance for what you consider inappropriate spending. Reduce another privilege if you feel you must do something.

You may think blowing a $2 allowance on five packs of baseball cards is a waste. Within an eight-year-old's culture, however, those cards are very important. You must give your child leeway to spend as he wants. When you do, you help build trust, self-reliance, and experience.

Be willing to hold your children responsible for living within their budget. Some weeks they may have to go without, particularly when they run out of money.

An allowance is a vital tool for teaching children how to budget, save, and make their own decisions. Children remember and learn from mistakes when their own money is lost or spent foolishly.

Model the Proper Use of Credit

In today's society we see the results of individuals and couples using bad judgment regarding credit.

Explain to your children why it is necessary to use credit and the importance of paying back their loan on a timely basis. You can make this a great teaching tool. Give them practice in filling out credit forms. Their first loan might be from you to them for a special purchase. Go through all the mechanics that a bank would do: Fill out a credit application and sign a paper with all the information stated. Let them understand about interest, installment payments, balloon payments, late payment costs, etc. Teach them to be responsible to pay on time.

Teach Your Children How to Save

In today's instant society, it is hard to teach this lesson. At times we should deny our children certain material things so they have a reason to save. As they get older they will want bicycles, stereos, a car, a big trip, etc. They can relate to establishing the habit of saving with these larger items.

One of the first ways to begin teaching the concept of savings is to give the children some form of piggy bank. This way spare change or extra earnings can go into the piggy bank. When the bank gets full, you might want to open an account at the local bank.

When they are older you might want to establish a passbook account at the local bank so they can go to the bank and personally deposit to their account.

In the end, children who learn how to save will better appreciate what they have worked to acquire.

If you can, reward your children for saving: "If you save half the money you need for a new bike, I'll give you the other half."

Show Them How to Be Wise in Their Spending

Take your children with you when you shop, and do some cost comparisons. They will soon see that with a little effort they can save a lot of money. You might want to demonstrate this in a tangible way when they want to purchase a larger item for themselves. Go to several stores looking for that one item, writing down the highest and the lowest price for the same item. Let them choose which one they want to purchase, and pay them the difference between what they chose and the most expensive. This way they can really see the savings.

Clothes is an area where a lot of lessons on wise spending can be made. After awhile they realize that designer clothes cost a lot more for that label or patch. Our daughter, Jenny, soon learned that outlet stores were great bargains for clothes dollars. To this day she can still find excellent bargains by comparison shopping.

Let Children Work Part-Time

There are many excellent part-time jobs available for your child. Fast food outlets, markets, malls, babysitting, etc., give valuable work experience to your children. Some entrepreneurial youngsters even begin a thriving business around their skills and interest. These part-time jobs are real confidence boosters. Just remember to keep a proper balance between work, home, church, and school. A limit of 10 to 15 hours per week might be a good guideline. Much more than that will affect a proper balance.

Let Them Help You with Your Budgeting

Encourage your children to help you budget and pay for the family finances. This gives them experience in real-life money problems. They also get a better idea about your family's financial income and expenses. Children's ideas are good when it comes to suggestions or how to better utilize the family finances. This will give them a better understanding of why your family can't afford certain luxuries.

Give Them Experience in Handling Adult Expenses

As your children get older they need to experience real-life costs. Since children live at home, they don't always share in true-to-life expenses. Let them experience paying for their own telephone, car expenses, and clothing. Depending on the situation, help in paying a portion of the utility and household bills can be an invaluable experience for children who have finished school but are still living at home.

Give to the Lord

At a very young stage in life, parents and children should talk about where things come from. The children should be aware that all things are given from God and that He is just letting us borrow them for a time. Children can understand that we are to return back to God what He has so abundantly given to us. This principle can be experienced either through their Sunday school or through church offerings. When special projects at church come up, you might want to review the need with your children so they can decide if they want to give extra money above what they normally give to their church. Early training in this area gives a valuable basis for learning how to be a giver in life and not a taker.

Your children will learn about money from you, so be a good model. As they get older they will imitate what you do. If you have good habits, they will reflect that. If you struggle with finances, so will they. One valuable lesson to teach is that money doesn't necessarily reflect love. A hug, a smile, a kiss, or time spent together is much more valuable than money.

▲ Be sure to give your daughter the same experience with money as you do your son.

▲ For children whose parents are divorced, it can be helpful for the allowance to come from the nonresidential parent. The child will feel he is getting nurturing from that parent even though he isn't there, and this can provide built-in communication, even if it comes through the mail with a letter.

▲ Professionals do agree that the earlier you give children experience with money, the better.

$ It's Not Too Young $
to Start Saving

Let all things be done decently and in order.
—1 Corinthians 14:40 NKJV

In our first section we outlined how to organize a plan for your life which included teaching your children how to schedule a plan for their own lives.

If you have a teenager and are wondering if he or she will ever save a dime, you may want to look again at an IRA (Individual Retirement Account)—not for yourself, but as a way of assisting your children to a comfortable retirement.

Suppose your children start working as teenagers from a summer job; you can put $2000 per year of those earnings into an IRA, and reimburse your children with spending money. In return, there is a $2000 deduction on your child's tax return.

Do this for seven years until they are in their mid-twenties; then sit back and watch the fund grow.

If the IRA produces a 10 percent annual return for the next 40 years, the account will grow to over $600,000 when your child turns 65.

Even if the child doesn't earn the full $2000 to contribute, he could start with $500. Invest whatever he makes, whether small or large.

There are a couple of negatives to consider:

▲ The child can't use the money for college unless he or she withdraws it and pays a 10 percent penalty, plus taxes.

▲ The child can't start withdrawing penalty-free until age 59½. (However, there are several exceptions to this rule. See a tax adviser who is knowledgeable about IRA's.)

Discuss these limitations so you will realize the advantages and disadvantages. In most cases, if you put money in a IRA and let it grow for ten years, then withdraw it, you are ahead of the game even after paying the 10 percent penalty.

$ Teach Your Children $ How to Budget

Children learn more from what is caught than what is taught. Mom and Dad must set the proper example for planning for financial freedom. Children must learn that we don't spend everything we earn. Along with adults, they must learn to plan for the future, and one of the best ways to do this is to have a budget just like Mom and Dad. Children love to parrot their parents, so why not teach them about budgets?

Their budgets won't be as complicated or have as many items as yours, but the basic principles are the same. You will want to consider the following principles.

1. Keep It Simple

For a young child you might have only three categories: *saving, giving, and spending*. As a child reaches the teen years he or she will be breaking down these basic categories into subheadings, which will further break down into various priorities for each heading. Purchase of clothes is a big consideration as children get older. We took this period to teach our children about bargains, labels, value, and advertising. When they bought their clothes with their own money, they were more receptive to stretching their money as far as it would go.

College years develop your children into young adults, with many more subcategories being added to their budget. We believe firmly that these years are extremely important for your children to learn how to prioritize their limited resources. We also believe firmly that college-age students need to work part-time when in school. It should not be a time where everything is given to them. Vital choices will be made—some good and some not so good. However, the results of these choices will be very valuable as your children move into the real world.

2. Let the Budget Reflect the Child's Desires

One of the hardest challenges is to train your children to be independent and responsible for their decisions. Budget planning gives them practice in doing this. They are able to see in black and white how they are going to earn their money and how they are going to spend their money. If you want to read more in this area and would like samples of worksheets for your children, read Ron and Judy Blue's book *Money Matters for Parents and Their Kids*, published by Oliver Nelson. This is an excellent book full of valuable information.

3. Each Child and Each Age Group Has Unique Needs

No one budget will be adequate for all children and all age groups. As you work with your individual children you will begin to sense their uniqueness.

A budget isn't set in concrete; it is only a guide to let you list how you are going to spend your resources according to your predetermined priorities. If your goals and priorities change, then your budget will change to reflect those changes.

We all learn by mistakes. Give your children this freedom by allowing them the necessary practice to learn about budgets and how they work. When they learn this skill and apply it, it will become a habit that will carry over into adulthood.

This experience will help to prepare your children for a lifetime of financial freedom.

The worksheet on the next page will show you how to break down income and expenses. The child can easily put in the figures to work with (use a pencil because you will probably need to erase several times until it balances). As the children get older you can expand the form to include more information and categories.

Name _____

Activity Period _____

CHILDREN'S BUDGET WORKSHEET

INCOME	WEEKLY	MONTHLY
Allowance	$_____	$_____
Gifts	$_____	$_____
Outside work	$_____	$_____
Other	$_____	$_____
Total Income	$_____	$_____

EXPENSES		
Saving (10%)	$_____	$_____

Giving

Tithe (10%)	$_____	$_____
Gifts	$_____	$_____
Other	$_____	$_____

Spending

Clothes	$_____	$_____
Food	$_____	$_____
Music	$_____	$_____
Hobbies	$_____	$_____
Entertainment	$_____	$_____
School	$_____	$_____
Other	$_____	$_____
Total Expenses	$_____	$_____
*Extra monies left over	$_____ +	$_____ +
*Short monies	$_____ –	$_____ –

_____

*With extra money ask, "Where should this money go?" With a shortage of money ask, "What are you going to adjust or eliminate?"

$ Children Need to Be $
Good Shoppers Too

When your children are young, they need to go to the markets, malls, auctions, and yard sales with you to see how Mom and Dad purchase things for the family and themselves. They need to learn the process that goes through your mind before you purchase. Let them see how you select the items you buy. Is your decision-making purely impulsive, or does it fit into an overall pattern of planning?

Children learn to be wise shoppers by seeing how the adults in their lives purchase goods. Take the time to give them insight by avoiding impulse purchases.

- ▲ Never use a credit card to purchase anything on impulse.
- ▲ Never buy on impulse. Wait several days after you think about the item. Do I really need that?
- ▲ After deciding to go back and buy that impulsive item, share with a close friend why and how you made that decision.
- ▲ Go to a person to whom you can be accountable and discuss this purchase with him or her.

You might say, "This is really a slow process; I'll never get anything done!" The whole attempt is to discourage you and your children from being impulsive buyers.

You need to give your children two very important permissions: *counsel* and then *freedom* to make mistakes. Let them know that you are always available to help them out and that it's okay to make mistakes with money. With each mistake we hope there is a lesson learned. The important lesson is that they learn to manage money their way, not your way.

We used our Family Conference Time to help our children learn about many things, but in particular *money*. (See pages 161-167 in *Survival for Busy Women* for more information regarding Family Conference Time.) Many topics and decisions were made for the total family and individuals within the family. Many of our times were spent discussing how to be good and smart shoppers, particularly after one of the members either ran out of money, paid too much for an item, or bought inferior quality.

Some of our thoughts were:

▲ Seek advice from other members of the family.

▲ Watch for sales.

▲ Find out where the manufacturer outlets are located.

▲ Don't take credit cards with you unless you have established the habit of paying off the balance at the end of each month.

▲ Take a predetermined shopping list with you.

▲ Set a dollar limit on what you can spend.

▲ Live by your budget for the week and month.

▲ Buy quality (the cost per wearing is more important).

▲ Use discipline not to browse; seek out only those things on your list.

▲ Ponder the purchase; dwell on your decision. Make sure that you really need that item. Many times you decide you really don't need it right now.

▲ Wait two days on an impulse purchase.

▲ Take an inventory of your clothes to see what you have too much of and what you might need in order to complement your basic wardrobe. (See Exhibit T in *Survival for Busy Women* for a chart to help you with your wardrobe inventory.)

▲ If you have an older brother or sister (son or daughter), see if he or she has some good clothes to sell to another member of the family.

Learning how to buy wisely is not easy in an affluent society. In many communities this isn't even a popular topic. Yet we need to teach this character trait to our children at a very young age.

Children can help with maintenance and repairs in order to learn how to be good stewards. This teaches them two valuable lessons:

▲ How to make repairs around the home. They learn carpentry, plumbing, electrical work, landscaping, etc.

▲ How to properly take care of things so they last longer.

You are the role model, so evaluate yourself. Maybe you need to improve the mirror before you can expect your children to reflect what they see in it.

$ Children Can Have Fun $ Earning Money

Children are a gift from God; they are his reward.
—Psalm 127:3 TLB

As our children grew up we thought up all kinds of ways to create money-earning ventures. One of the very first projects they did was at ages five and six. We lived in a beach area in Southern California and spent time collecting shells and rocks. We had so many that they overflowed the bedrooms. So one summer the kids and Emilie had a rock-painting session in the garage with acrylic paints. They made creative colorful rocks and shells, and when they were finished my son and daughter displayed their creations in their wagon and walked the neighborhood selling their rocks and shells for 5 cents each. They were so excited to trade rocks and shells for cash.

It's hard for children to earn money doing chores around the house. Even for money it just isn't the same as earning it for themselves. When children earn money for themselves it builds self-reliance and gives them a sense of responsibility. When the jobs are fun and helpful, everyone benefits.

How much should Mom and Dad be involved? Plenty at first. Make sure you know the people who are hiring your child. Help match your child's age and ability to the job in question, and be sure the child is realistically paid for his or her time. After that, pull back, relax, and watch your child blossom with the satisfaction of earning money for a job well done.

Over the years we have come up with many money-making ideas, all family tested, that *work*! Here they are.

1. Toy sale. This children's version of the garage sale works especially well when the prices are kept low, since most customers will be other children. Stick price tags on everything, post a sign at the bottom of the driveway, and place the most eye-catching items up front. Let the children take it from there. They will learn about making change, negotiating, and, after sitting for hours between customers, perseverance.

2. Pet sitting. Many owners of birds, cats, and goldfish (and other pets that don't need walking) hire a sitter to come in every day to feed the animals, change what needs changing, and give the pets some love and affection. Depending on the child's age, you may have to help lock and unlock the pet owner's doors or gates. But once inside, it's the child's job, and it's a good one. Standard rates of pay for this service are between $1.50 and $4 per day.

3. Yardwork. Even before they're old enough to handle power equipment, children can help garden in other ways. Their young backs don't get nearly as tired from pulling weeds and planting flowers as adults' backs do, and children make great scouts for hidden rocks and branches that play havoc with the lawn mower. Rates should be a penny per rock for the tiny tots and more when the work is harder.

4. Dog walking. The size of the dog may dictate the size of the walker, but most kids can handle this job. People are surprisingly eager to pay someone else to walk their dog, especially when the weather is sloppy. Today's busy person is usually happy to pay $1 per walk.

5. Assisting at children's birthday parties. The hired helper should be only a few years older than the party group. He can help pass out food, round up trash and wrapping paper, oversee the games, and provide a vital extra set of eyes and hands for those guests who wander off and search for something breakable. Rate of pay: $3 per party.

6. Cleaning out crawl spaces, storage sheds, etc. The more cramped the space the better little bodies can help to clean it. Children are surprisingly strong and endlessly curious about cluttered nooks and crannies. Though they can't sort through the things you've accumulated, it may be worth paying a few cents just for the company. Rate of pay: $.50 per hour.

7. Child walking. An older child can walk a younger child to school every day, to a music lesson, or to the playground for a time of teeter-totter or swinging. Estimated rate of pay: $.25 per day.

8. Summer stock. This is always a fun time for children to express their talents. Plan a show where several children put on an act or talent show. Sing a song or lip sync to a record, tell a few jokes, play an instrument, juggle, write and then read a poem, do a dance, or teach the dog a trick and then have the dog do tricks. Sell tickets to the show. Suggested ticket price: $.20 to $.50 each, depending on the talents.

9. Summer camp. This is great fun for several children to help in. Together they can supervise up to eight children—making crafts, running relay races, conducting a story read-aloud hour.

Two hours is usually the maximum attention span for most children. Rates should be from $2 to $4 per child, depending on the cost of craft items necessary, such as Popsicle sticks, yarn, paints, cookies, juice, and other goodies.

10. Spook house. This is a great idea for the neighborhood children. A young imagination and some old sheets can turn a basement or garage into a spook house. Tunnels can be made with sheets and special effects created with all kinds of music and stuffed animals popping up and jumping out. Admission: 5 cents per child. Some kids will come back again and again.

11. Car wash. This is always a hit. Cloths, a whisk broom, buckets, soap, and window spray will be the equipment needed. Children can go door to door and make appointments. Timing is important. After the winter weather has thawed out and the spring rains are over is a good time to canvass the neighborhood. If they do a good job your children could turn this into a weekly event. Rates range from $1.50 to $3 per car, depending on the size of the car and how well the job is done.

12. House-sitting. Many people like their homes taken care of when out of town or on vacation. This is a good opportunity for the child to learn responsibility. The lawn and potted outdoor plants need watering, paper and mail need to be taken inside, indoor plants need to be watered, and lights need to be turned on and off to make the situation seem normal. Pets can also be fed and watered. The rate of pay will depend on the amount of work done. Range: $1 to $5 per day.

PART SEVEN

Good Consumer, Good Manager

▲ ▲ ▲

$ Supermarket Savings Waiting to Be Had $

T oday in our busy society we find that much of our stress is caused by how we provide nutrition for our family. At one time there was much emphasis upon family spending quality time around the family dining room table. Many times in years gone by we could expect to have at least two of the three meals (breakfast and dinner) together.

Much of the quality time was spent around the table. This was a great place to have a "summit conference" or just to catch up on the day's happenings. Today with our hustled, hassled, and hurried society we have stopped or seriously neglected this tradition. I encourage each family to seriously consider and evaluate their family time and see if at least one meal can be shared together. If you do make this commitment, try to make this a pleasant time for the family. This is not the time to be negative; make it an uplifting time, one where all members want to get back together again.

Many busy families have surrendered to the fast food phenomenon and very rarely cook at home. Fast food is fine occasionally, but should be viewed cautiously for regular meals. Those who find themselves on tight budgets will soon find this compromise most expensive, and in many cases it deprives your family of balanced nutrition.

Don't view food preparation as drudgery, but a delight in providing meals for your family. There are excellent cookbooks available that simplify food preparation. To ease your meals you might make up 3x5 cards giving you about seven different recipes for breakfast, lunch, and dinner. By rotating them, you can have a variety and not get bored with your meals. Try to introduce a new recipe occasionally. If you have teenagers, they can be of great assistance in this area. They can set the table, shop, clean vegetables, start the meal, serve the food, clean the table, and even load the dishwasher. This is an excellent opportunity to teach your children many lessons of adult life: meal planning, shopping for bargains, budget preparation, nutritional balance, table etiquette, time management in cooking meals, and cleaning up the mess.

Emilie has a friend who took one summer to teach her teenage sons how to survive, she called it "Survival Summer." At the end of the summer she felt comfortable that her boys could take care of themselves in an emergency. An added benefit is that she now has help with her ever-expanding responsibilities.

One word of caution is that busy teenagers carrying a heavy college prep academic load must have time for their studies. However, this doesn't mean they shouldn't carry some responsibilities for the family functions.

To help you save money at the supermarket I have listed several helpful hints for you. These should not only make shopping more efficient, but should also save you money.

1. Shop with a purpose and with a list. Plan your menus for the entire week (or two) and then organize your shopping list so that you have to pass through each section of the supermarket only once. You might even make a list of standard products, arranged to correspond to the flow of your normal shopping market. (See the sample marketing list at the end of this chapter.) If you have to return to the first aisle to pick up just one thing, you may find yourself attracted by other items. Stay away from impulsive buying. This will push you over your food budget and cause you added stress.

2. Try to control your impulse buying. Studies have estimated that almost 50 percent of purchases are entirely unplanned (not on your list). Be especially careful at the start of your shopping trip, when your cart is nearly empty. You're more susceptible to high-priced, unplanned purchases at that time.

3. Get your shopping done within a half-hour. This means you don't shop at "rush hour" time. Stay away from this hour; it will hurry you up and you will have a greater tendency to just pull off items from the shelves without really comparatively shopping for the best product. Supermarkets are often very comfortable places to linger in, but one study suggests that customers spend at least 50 cents a minute after a half-hour in the store.

4. Shop alone if you can. Children and even spouses cause us to compromise our lists. They try to help us with unplanned purchases. Television advertising causes great stress when our children go with us. They want to make sure they have the latest cereal, even though it is loaded with sugar and has very little nutritional value.

5. Never shop when hungry. Enough said. The psychology is obvious.

6. Use coupons wisely. Food companies often use coupon offers to promote either new products or old products that haven't been selling well. Ask yourself if you would have bought the item had there been no coupon, and compare prices with competing brands to see if you're really saving money. (See Chapter 46 for more details.)

7. Be a smart shopper. Be aware that grocery stores stock the highest-priced items at eye level. The lower-priced staples like flour, sugar, and salt are often below eye level, as are bulk quantities of many items.

There are more and more specialty stores that carry bulk food items. They can give you excellent cost savings if you are buying for a large family or are joint purchasing for several families or even for a picnic. One word of caution is that even though you might save money on bulk buying, you might really spend more because your family doesn't consume the item fast enough, and it spoils. This waste can be expensive.

Also, be aware that foods displayed at the end of an aisle may appear to be on sale, but often are not.

8. Use unit pricing. Purchase a small pocket calculator to take with you to the market. This way you can take the price or the item and divide by the number of units to find the per-unit cost. This way you can compare apples with apples. The listed price is not always the cheapest price.

9. Avoid foods that are packaged as individual servings. Extra packaging usually boosts the price of the product. This becomes too expensive for families. In some cases a one- or two-member family might be able to buy this way, but most families would not find this an economical way to purchase food.

10. When buying meat consider the amount of lean meat in the cut as well as the price per pound. A relatively high-priced cut with little or no waste may provide more meat for your money than a low-priced cut with a great deal of bone, gristle, or fat. Chicken, turkey, and fish are often good bargains for the budget buyer.

11. Buy vegetables and fruits in season, since they will be at their peak of quality and their lowest price. Never buy the first crop; prices are sure to go down later. You might even want to consider planning an "old-time canning weekend." This gives you the greatest economy and lets you enjoy these delicacies all during the year.

As an informed consumer you need to become more and more aware of what the labels on your products mean. Remember that manufacturers need to add additives and preservatives to give color and longer shelf life to their products. As a buyer you may not be willing to make that trade-off. There are a lot of natural foods on the market which can protect your family from the side effects of additives. The labels can tip you off as to what's in the jar or the carton.

What Food Labels Tell You

▲ **Ingredients**. Ingredients must be listed in descending order of prominence by weight. The first ingredients listed are the main ingredients in that product.

▲ **Color and flavors**. Added colors and flavors do not have to be listed by name, but the use of artificial colors or flavors must be indicated.

▲ **Serving content**. For each serving: the serving size; the number of calories per serving; the amount of protein, carbohydrates, and fat in a serving; the percentage of the U.S. Recommended Daily Allowance (USRDA) for protein, and seven important vitamins and minerals.

▲ **Optional information.** Some labels also contain the following: the percentage of the USRDA for any of 12 additional vitamins and minerals; the amount of saturated and unsaturated fat and cholesterol in a serving; and the amount of sodium furnished by a serving.

What Food Labels Don't Tell You

▲ **What standardized foods contain**. Over 350 foods, including common ones like enriched white bread and catsup, are classified as "standardized," for which the FDA has established guidelines. Manufacturers are not required to list ingredients for these products.

▲ **How much sugar is in some products**. Sugar and sweeteners come in a variety of forms (white sugar, brown sugar, corn syrup, dextrose, sucrose, maltose, corn sweeteners), and if they're all listed separately, it's nearly impossible to know the true amount of sugar contained in a labeled product.

▲ **How "natural" a product is.** The FDA's policy on using the word "natural" on a food label is loose. The product may, in fact, be highly processed and full of additives.

▲ **Specific ingredients that may be harmful**. Since coloring or spices that don't have to be listed by name can cause nausea, dizziness, or hives in certain people, people with food or additive allergies don't know which products they need to avoid.

An informed shopper has more control over his or her purchase style and habits. Much of your budget money goes to food. Become a good steward of God's money and get the most in return for that money.

SHOPPING LIST

DATE _MAY 5_

Qty. Cost   **Qty. Cost**   **Qty. Cost**

STAPLES

	Qty.	Cost
Cereal	—	—
Flour	—	—
Jello	—	—
Mixes	—	—
Nuts	—	—
Stuffing	—	—
Sugar	—	—

SPICES

	Qty.	Cost
Bacon Bits	—	—
Bak. Powder	—	—
Chocolate	—	—
Coconut	—	—
Salt/Pepper	✓	—
Soda	—	—

PASTA

	Qty.	Cost
Inst. Potato	—	—
Mixes	—	—
Pasta	✓	—
Rice	—	—
Spaghetti	✓	—

DRINKS

	Qty.	Cost
Apple Cider	✓	—
Coffee	—	—
Juice	✓	—
Sparkling	✓	—
Tea	—	—

CANNED GOODS

	Qty.	Cost
Canned Fruit	—	—
Strawberry	(1)	—
	—	—
	—	—
	—	—
Canned Meals	—	—
Canned Meat	—	—
Canned Vegetables	—	—
	—	—
	—	—
Soups		
Chicken	1	—
	—	—
Tuna	3	—

CONDIMENTS

	Qty.	Cost
Catsup	1	—
Honey	—	—
Jelly/Jam	1	—
Mayonnaise	—	—
Molasses	—	—
Mustard	—	—
Oil	—	—
Peanut Butter	1	—
Pickles	—	—
Relish	—	—
Salad Dressing	1	—
Shortening	—	—
Syrup	—	—
Tomato Paste	—	—
Tomato Sauce	—	—
Vinegar	—	—

PAPER GOODS

	Qty.	Cost
Foil	—	—
Napkins	—	—
Paper Towels	—	—
Plastic Wrap	1	—
Tissues	—	—
Toilet Paper	—	—
Toothpicks	—	—
Trash Bags	—	—
Waxed Paper	—	—
Zip Bags		
Small	—	—
Large	1	—

HOUSEHOLD

	Qty.	Cost
Bleach	—	—
Clothes Soap	—	—
Dish Soap	—	—
Dishwasher Soap	—	—
Fab. Softener	1	—
Furn. Polish	—	—
Light Bulbs	—	—
Pet Food	—	
Vacuum Bags	—	

FRESH PRODUCE

	Qty.	Cost
Fruit Apple	6	
Oranges	6	
banana	4	
Vegetables		
celery	1	
lettuce	1	

PERSONAL ITEMS

	Qty.	Cost
Body Soap	—	—
Deodorant	1	—
Fem. Protection	—	—
Hair Care	—	—
Make Up	—	—
	—	—
	—	—
	—	—

FROZEN FOOD/JUICE

	Qty.	Cost
Ice Cream	—	—
	—	—
	—	—
Juice		
Orange	✓	—
Pineapple	✓	—
T.V. Dinners	—	—
	—	—
	—	—
Vegetables	—	—
	—	—
	—	—
	—	—

PASTRY

	Qty.	Cost
Bread/s	2	—
Buns	—	—
Chips	—	—
Cookies	—	—
Crackers	1	—
Croutons	—	—

MEAT

	Qty.	Cost
Beef	—	—
	—	—
	—	—
Chicken	3	—
	—	—
	—	—

DAIRY

	Qty.	Cost
Butter	1	—
Cheese	1#	—
Cottage Ch	1	—
Eggs	12	—
Milk	1Q	—
Sour Cream	—	—

EXHIBIT Q

$ We Give Double $
Coupons Today

A good wife watches for bargains.

—From Proverbs 31:18 TLB

Many smart women are saving money by couponing; today's household is certainly concerned with finances!

Emilie talked with several women who are a part of a "Coupon Club" in their church. They meet monthly to exchange coupons and rebate forms.

They have a well-organized file system for their coupons. They bring in magazines and newspapers given to them by other people, so the time can be spent in cutting out coupons and filing away or exchanging with each other.

Emilie has found that an accordion 9″ x 5½″ file is a great tool for organizing coupons. Your topics may include:

- ▲ Personal/health
- ▲ Laundry
- ▲ Poultry/meats
- ▲ Cereals
- ▲ Baby
- ▲ Dairy
- ▲ Breads
- ▲ Garden

- ▲ Mixes
- ▲ Frozen
- ▲ Cleaners
- ▲ Baking products
- ▲ Soda pop
- ▲ Dry goods
- ▲ Snacks
- ▲ Cookies

▲ Charcoal
▲ Soups
▲ Sauces
▲ Rice
▲ Lunch meats
▲ Paper products

▲ Salad/seasoning
▲ Package mixes
▲ Jams
▲ Coffee/tea
▲ Miscellaneous

When cutting out a coupon, run a yellow highlighter pen over the expiration date. That way your eye will catch the date quickly.

I met a special young mother who told me she saved $850 last year by couponing. Another working woman saved $1100 couponing in one year.

These women struck my interest, and I asked them to share with me some of the ideas that helped save them that kind of money. Here are some of those ideas:

▲ A store will run a special ad in the local newspaper—for example, coffee for $1.99. You have a coffee coupon for 50¢ off. This week you also cut out a coupon that entitles you to a double discount on any coupon. You then can purchase that $1.99 can of coffee for only 99¢.

▲ Whenever possible use double coupons. If your market is not honoring double coupons, it could be worth driving to another local market that does, so you can get the double discount on your coupons.

▲ You can cut out coupons for "luxury" items (freezer baggies, expensive brand of disposable diapers, pie crust mix, etc.) and many times end up finding these things on a clearance table, either discontinued by the market or manufacturer or else damaged. With your coupon doubled you can get it free or at a minimal price. (A mix for rye bread, clearance priced at $.90 with a $.40 doubled coupon, cost me $.10.)

▲ On items you use a lot that are costly (disposable diapers, soda pop, or coffee) drive to another neighborhood market for a great deal. The savings are worth it, so stock up as much as your budget and number of double coupons will allow. When a meat item is priced well, stock up on it. If you eat a lot of poultry and prefer breast meat only, go elsewhere to save $.60 to $.70 a pound, and stock up as much as you can. Because you can stock up, you won't have to do this very often. Also, there are many poultry coupons available; double them and enjoy more savings.

▲ What is hard to understand is that in double couponing the *smaller* quantity is usually the better buy because you can get it for a few cents, if not free. Just buy two or three dish detergents, and you'll have enough until another brand goes on special.

▲ Switch brands of most items regularly. Couponing lets you try lots of products. Obviously there are some things you won't care for, so don't buy them again. But on the average you can switch peanut butter, jelly, rice, margarine, coffee, soda pop, paper towels, toilet paper, etc. You might find a better product in the sampling. Because of couponing, generic is *not* always the best buy. If you can get a superior product for the same price, or usually less, then use the coupon. Stock up on staples and paper products. (If you don't have very much storage, you can put things in the garage or even under the beds.)

▲ Most important is getting hold of coupons and filing them. Throw *nothing* away, even if you get two major papers on Thursday, food section day! Tucked into our PennySaver (a throwaway neighborhood advertising paper) is Safeway's advertising circular. Our market is currently doubling *all* other markets' coupons, so we cut out Safeway's and keep them for that week. Friends and neighbors can even give you leftover coupons that are mailed to them. You can use many of these as well. However, go through your file once or twice a month to discard those which have gone beyond their expiration date.

▲ Refunding is complicated, or can be, so you'll want to set up rules for yourself. Get all refunding forms from newspapers or magazines because most markets don't stock them. Don't buy the required number of products *unless* you have the refund form. (It's easy to have the advertiser say the refund form is available at your grocer's, but it rarely is.) Try to combine your refunds with purchasing the item on sale, with a doubled coupon, or better, both! It must be something you use often, and not a new, untried product (who wants three boxes of terrible-tasting cereal with another free one on the way?). Many people save all box tops and wrappings. We have tried this and found that it simply was not worth it to us. Most refunds are for combinations of foods we don't buy or use. Therefore, wait until you see the requirements and then decide if it is worth the effort and postage. Our guidelines don't allow us to refund for less than $1, and even then the purchase must be on sale or a coupon must be used.

Where can you get coupons? Many places—a lot come through the mail. We used to throw out junk mail and not even look at it. Now we quickly finger through the pages and cut out the coupons, then toss the rest.

Major and local newspapers run coupons every week.

Have friends cut coupons and save them for you. Our Auntie cuts coupons. It gives her a purpose to help, plus any she doesn't use she passes on to us, and any we don't use we then pass on to our married daughter, Jenny.

Grandmas and grandpas can have this couponing as a great project.

Neighbors, friends, relatives, and old magazines are a great source of coupons.

Cutting out, filing, and organizing will take you no more than ½ hour per week but can easily save you $13 to $20 per week on your grocery bill. This pays you four to six times the minimum wage.

Try it; you'll love it. It's another way of being a good steward of your money.

How to Cut Your Family's Medical Bills

If you are untrustworthy about worldly wealth, who will trust you with the true riches of heaven?

—Luke 16:11 TLB

If your health insurance rates are like our family's, they're getting bigger and bigger each year. Since we aren't covered by a group plan, we have our own private carrier, and each year the renewal premium has increased. In order to keep the premiums somewhat manageable, we have increased our deductible, knowing that our biggest concerns are coverage for major medical costs.

There are several ways to control medical expenses.[1]

Doctors

▲ Don't see a specialist if you don't have to. A general practitioner will be able to handle most problems, and his rates are usually less than those of the specialist.

▲ Don't go to the emergency room if you can go to the doctor's office instead.

▲ Consider your physician as a partner in your health care. Ask any questions you have. Don't be afraid to ask that silly question.

▲ Get advice from your doctor over the phone if you need clarification or information on such things as medications, reactions, or recurring health problems. You don't need an office visit to have something explained.

▲ Get a second opinion on anything major, such as surgery. A high percentage of second opinions don't verify the initial diagnosis.

▲ Don't overtest. Find out what alternatives you have if you refuse the test.

▲ Consider negotiating fees with your doctor. Doctors are usually willing to work out a fee and payment schedule for their services.

▲ In order to stagger the cost of health care, sequentially schedule the medical and dental checkups of the family members.

Hospitals

▲ Don't have procedures done as an inpatient that can be done as an outpatient.

▲ Ask for an itemized bill. Question what you don't understand. It helps if you can keep your own records of what you received and when.

▲ Pay your bill only after checking it over. Make sure all questions are reviewed.

▲ You can curtail hospital expenses if you try to avoid being admitted on a Friday. Friday admissions result in longer stays than admissions on another day. For the shortest stay, try to have yourself admitted on a Tuesday.

A federal law (effective December 1, 1991), called the *Patient Self-Determination Act*, requires hospitals and other health care providers to give you information (when you're admitted) about your rights to accept or refuse medical treatment, and to prepare a document that will authorize someone else to make decisions for you.

You can also get help in deciphering your hospital bills, and information on where to file complaints, by joining *People's Medical Society* (462 Walnut Street, Allentown, PA 18102, 215-770-1670, $15 a year membership fee), a consumer's advocacy organization.

Equipment

▲ Borrow medical equipment (such as canes or wheelchairs) that you may need only a short time. If you can't borrow, see if renting would be cheaper than buying. If you must buy, see whether your insurance will pay for the purchase. Check for sales. Buy only equipment with a written warranty.

Nursing Care

▲ Use home nursing care as an alternative to long-term nursing home care if possible. Staying at home is far less expensive than staying in a nursing home. Other possibilities include adult daycare and respite care, in which family members get a break by using a paid caregiver for a set time each week.

Medicine

▲ Buy generic drugs when possible. They are usually cheaper and just as effective. There are a few situations where it's important to get a brand name drug, so consult your doctor.

Generic drugs, which have the same formulation as the more expensive name brand drugs, are far less expensive, but even *their* prices vary. Large pharmacy chains and hospital outpatient pharmacies will probably be your best bargain. Shop around and buy the largest quantities advisable to get the best discount.

▲ Buy in bulk if you use regular medication. Be sure to check the shelf life of such purchases.

▲ Sometimes a mail-order service can save you money.

You can save as much as 20 percent less by ordering prescription drugs by mail. Their prices vary, so here are four companies to telephone:

▲ *Action-Mail Order*:	800-452-1976
▲ *Medi-Mail*:	800-331-1458
▲ *Family Pharmaceuticals*:	800-922-3444
▲ *Pharmail*:	800-237-8927

If you're a veteran, also check with your local Veterans Administration Office for their mail-order program. As a veteran, if you meet certain requirements, try the Department of Veterans Affairs, which operates a large mail-prescription service.

For those 55 and older, the American Association of Retired Persons, through its affiliated organization, Retired Persons Services, Inc., offers a mail-order pharmacy service for members and their families. Details: 800-456-4636, 8 A.M. to 6 P.M. weekdays, 9 A.M. to noon on Saturday. Or check your medical insurance company.

Whether you get your prescription in person or by mail, make sure you've gotten the right medication, strength, and directions. Also check the expiration date.

▲ Buy store brands when you have no strong preference. Aspirin is aspirin. It is usually made by one of the same companies in any case.

▲ If your local pharmacist isn't competitive, you might mention this to him for a possible savings.

▲ Use over-the-counter drugs whenever possible. Ask your doctor and/or pharmacist for an over-the-counter medication if it will work well. Many prescription drugs are becoming available over-the-counter; check for changes.

▲ Get longer life out of your medicines by storing them properly.

▲ Over-the-counter and prescription drugs may perform miracles when they're *needed*. If they're *not*, we're wasting money and risking the side effects. Be sure to ask your doctor for the least expensive and safest prescription. Ask for free starter samples.

▲ If you have a chronic condition for which you need medication, have it reevaluated periodically. I took drops for glaucoma for years, until refinements in the screening tests revealed that I don't have glaucoma at all! Now I have my pressure checked annually, and all is well.

▲ Don't take too many vitamins and minerals unless you need them. If you're in good health, and eat a balanced diet, save your money.

Insurance

▲ Don't overpay on your insurance. Make sure you aren't duplicating your coverages and that you aren't carrying coverage you don't need (e.g., maternity coverage when you no longer can have children).

▲ Increase your deductible to save money.

▲ If you are a nonsmoker, look for a carrier that will give you a discount.

▲ Consider an HMO or prepaid health program.

▲ If your carrier requires preapproval, make sure you get it.

▲ Pay premiums annually if you can. Be sure to pay on time.

▲ Don't abuse your company's insurance policy. The higher the company's expenses, the higher the premium costs, which affect your company's profitability.

Prevention

▲ Exercise regularly.

▲ Eat proper foods, with reduced consumption of fats, sugars, sodium, fried foods, red meats, and high-cholesterol foods. (See Emilie's book *Eating Right* published by Harvest House.)

▲ Learn stress-reduction techniques.

▲ Injury-proof your home.

▲ Wear seatbelts.

▲ Be a nonsmoker.

▲ Be a nondrinker of alcoholic beverages.

▲ Take advantage of free or inexpensive community testing health fairs.

Medical Reference Books

Be an informed consumer and have some medical background. Listed below are some excellent medical reference books:

▲ *American Medical Association Family Medical Guide* (Random House, 1987). Simple diagnostic flow charts and illustrations, with suggestions of when to use home remedies and when a doctor is needed.

▲ *American Medical Association Handbook of First Aid* (Random House, 1987). If your first aid book is as old as mine *was*, you'll be surprised by the changes in AMA-recommended procedures. It's important to have up-to-date information.

▲ *Take Care of Yourself*, by Donald M. Vickery and James F. Fries (Addison-Wesley, 1990). Emphasizes self-care and prevention. Not as detailed as the AMA Guide, but a good supplement.

▲ *Prescription Drug Book*, 2nd ed., by AARP Pharmacy Service (Harper Perennial, 1992). Of special interest to those of us over 50.

▲ *The Complete Drug Reference*, by U.S. Pharmacopeial Convention, Inc. (Consumer Report Books, 1991). Very detailed, includes nonprescription drugs.

▲ *The Essential Guide to Prescription Drugs*, by James W. Long (Harper Collins, 1991). Not as detailed as the above, but the price is a lot better. Good description of drug treatment for specific conditions.

▲ *The Pill Book* (Bantam Books, 1991). This book is priced low, so it's worthwhile to keep each annual edition on your shelf. Brief, clear explanations of drugs.

▲ *Getting the Most for Your Medical Dollar*, by Charles Inlander (Pantheon, 1991).

▲ *The Patient's Guide to Medical Tests*, 3rd ed., by Edward and Kathy Pinckney, M.D. (Facts on File).

Fraud Alert

Swindlers in the health-care field now cost us between $50 and $80 billion a year—affecting our taxes and insurance premiums. A few safeguards:

▲ Check all your medical bills carefully for inaccuracies.

▲ Get recommendations from your doctor for home services or equipment.

▲ Don't trust door-to-door sales or telephone pitches.

▲ Beware of offers for free checkups and batteries of tests. If in doubt, check with your doctor or hospital.

▲ Don't get involved in any shady maneuvers promising you padded insurance deals.

▲ If you suspect fraud, contact your state's attorney general's office, or your insurance company. Medicare has a toll-free hotline for fraud reports: 800-368-5779 (or write HHS/OIG, P. O. Box 17303, Baltimore, MD 21203-7303).

$ **Ways to Stretch Your Dollars** $

I, wisdom, will make the hours of your day more profitable and the years of your life more fruitful.

—Proverbs 9:11 TLB

In today's economy we need to know as much as we can about tax laws and how to use tax deductions we have not employed in the past. This chapter will help you work within the law to stretch your dollar.

Here are a few techniques, rules, and suggestions to keep in mind.[1]

Tax-Saving Tips

▲ **Itemized deductions** can help reduce your tax bill, but watch out: You can only deduct miscellaneous deductions to the extent that they *equal or exceed 2 percent of your adjusted gross income.* You can only deduct medical expenses to the extent that they *equal or exceed 7.5 percent of your adjusted gross income* (don't forget to include transportation costs to your doctor at 9 cents per mile). But don't get too carried away with itemized deductions; you could be subject to the Alternative Minimum Tax.

▲ **Claim a deduction on Schedule C or Schedule F**, rather than on Schedule A, whenever possible. Not only will you be able to deduct 100 percent of the expense, but any deductions listed on Schedules C or F reduce your adjusted gross income, making it easier to meet the 2 percent miscellaneous and 7.5 percent medical deduction floors.

▲ **Business expense** deductions also give you a good deal of latitude. The IRS simply says they must be "ordinary and necessary." Don't overlook computer costs, supplies, subscription costs, seminar costs, etc.

▲ **Postpone income or bonus payments** until next year. Your company can still announce the amounts this year, but if payment is delayed until next year, you don't have to report it for the current year. Ask your company about exceptions.

▲ **Transfer income-producing property to low-bracket children or grandchildren.** Although children under 14 pay tax at their parents' rate above the first $1000, that $1000 can represent a fair amount of annual investment income. You could pay over $300 in taxes on it, but the youngster would pay only $75 (the standard deduction offsets any tax on the first $500; the next $500 is taxed at only 15 percent).

Ways to Minimize Taxes on Stocks and Bonds

▲ **Offset capital gains with capital losses.** Take investment losses the same year you claim gains. Such losses offset gains, and up to $3000 of ordinary income.

▲ **Give your favorite charity securities or other property that has gone up in value.** With a cash donation you merely get a deduction. But with an outright gift of an appreciated asset you deduct the full value *and* avoid capital gains tax.

▲ **Consider selling appreciated securities you bought on margin.** If you borrowed on margin, you are entitled to a deduction for loan interest to a $4000 limit, plus an amount equal to your net investment income. If you didn't realize enough gain to deduct all the interest paid out, consider selling some appreciated securities.

Exemptions That Can Lower Your Property Taxes

Exemptions for property tax vary from state to state, but there are several exemptions that are available in many states. Here are three that you may qualify for. (To find out more about the property tax exemptions for your state, call your local tax assessor.)

▲ Veterans often qualify for an exemption of $50 per year.

▲ A blind individual, or a surviving spouse of a blind individual, can get an exemption of up to $6000.

▲ A disabled veteran, or a surviving spouse of a disabled veteran, may be completely exempt from property taxes.

Note: For a surviving spouse to claim either of the last two exemptions, the spouse must live on the property and cannot remarry.

Maximizing Deductions to the Fullest

▲ **Pay off big loans (and the interest) with a home-equity loan.** The proceeds of up to a $100,000 loan can go for any legitimate purpose, and the loan interest is 100 percent tax-free.

▲ **Pre pay all local real estate taxes;** also, pay any estimated last-quarter income tax owed to the state or city for a deduction this year.

▲ **Turn dues into "professional expenses."** If you belong to a country club and use the club at least 50 percent of the time for business, you can deduct at least 80 percent of the expenses and 100 percent of the dues. Use the club for business lunches before New Year's Eve, or throw a "goodwill" lunch or dinner. Keep records to show that you talked business.

▲ **Increase medical deductions** so they exceed 7.5 percent of your adjusted gross income. Move up your annual physical from January to December, or pay the full amount for medical or dental procedures that start this year even if they aren't completed until next year. Stock up on your prescription drugs, medically prescribed vitamins and special diet foods (to the extent that they won't expire). Other deductions include the cost of a special mattress for arthritis or cosmetic surgery (even if not recommended by a physician); the cost of a program that prevents or alleviates a specific ailment; Medicare B premiums; room and board for an in-home nurse; the cost of orthopedic shoes; long-distance medical travel; psychotherapy; a home health spa; and computer storage of your medical history.

Three Types of Income That Require No Taxes

▲ **Gifts and inheritances** you receive are not usually taxable to you on the federal level, except for certain large amounts. (Some states have an inheritance tax.) The person making the gift/bequest has normally paid taxes, if any, on the income used to purchase the gift or to build the estate. However, income such as interest, dividends, or rents from such property is taxable.

▲ **Veterans Administration payments** and/or insurance proceeds aren't taxable.

▲ **Life insurance proceeds** paid at the death of the insured are usually tax-free, as are loans taken from a life insurance policy.

Gift-Giving As a Tax Relief Strategy

Want to make gifts that will please the recipients without giving you a nasty tax bite? Here are five ways to play angel without getting socked:

▲ **Cash gifts.** Give up to $10,000 per year per recipient in cash ($20,000 if the gift is from you and your spouse) and pay no gift tax.

▲ **U.S. savings bonds.** Consider a Series EE bond as a holiday gift. Unlike other zero coupon bonds, the tax on the annual increase in value of a Series EE is deferred until the holder cashes it in. But if the recipient of your gift is a young child, he or she may wish to report the tax annually. This could be a good idea if the amount is under $1000 and the child is in a low tax bracket; it might be better to pay a small tax each year than one big lump sum when the bond is sold.

▲ **Certificates of deposit.** Give your child or grandchild a bank CD in the child's name. Interest on a CD that matures in a year or less is taxable to the child at a lower rate when credited to the child's account.

▲ **Appreciated stock.** Give your child or grandchild stock that has gone up in value and thereby avoid capital gains tax yourself.

▲ **Charitable donations.** Donate something of value to a cherished alma mater or nonprofit organization.

Save Money on Your Travel Dollars

America seems to be on the go. Everyone is planning to go someplace—now or in the future. As Emilie and I are getting older and the children are grown, we have our eyes set on New England, the South, Mexico, Canada, Hawaii, Australia, and Tahiti.

When we were younger we had the time but not the money. Now we have the money but not the time!

Last year for Christmas I gave Emilie two gift certificates to be used anytime this year: One was for a week in Hawaii and one was for a week in Mexico. So far Hawaii is scheduled but not Mexico.

When we set out to travel we want some of the best rates available. We are always looking for a deal. This chapter is specifically written to help you find that good deal. If you are a senior citizen, be sure you let agencies know this when you make travel arrangements. This age group usually has special discounts.

Travel Tours

▲ **Aerotours International**—36 E. 3rd Street, New York, NY 10003, 800-223-4555, 212-979-5000. They offer resort apartment vacations to Australia, Fiji, Indonesia, the Philippines, and Tahiti.

▲ **American Youth Hostels**—P.O. Box 37613, Washington D.C. 20013, 202-783-6161. They can accommodate access to 5300 hostels in 59 countries. Senior citizens are welcome for a minimal annual membership fee.

▲ **Grandtravel**—6900 Wisconsin Avenue, Suite 706, Chevy Chase, MD 20815, 301-986-0790, 800-247-7651.

▲ **Grand Circle Travel**—347 Congress Street, Boston, MA 02210, 617-350-7500, 800-350-7500. International travel specializing in the 50+ age bracket.

▲ **Mayflower Tours**—1225 Warren Avenue, Downers Grove, IL 60515, 708-960-3430, 800-323-7604. This tour is designed for mature travelers specializing in U.S. sites.

▲ **Outdoor Vacations for Women Over 40**—P.O. Box 200, Groton, MA 01450, 508-448-3331. Outdoor travel adventures for women of all skill levels.

▲ **Saga Holidays Ltd.**—120 Boyston Street, Boston, MA 02116, 800-343-0273; 800-248-2234. Special low-priced travels for singles, grandparents and grandchildren, and those over 60 years old.

▲ **Untours**—Hal Taussig, Idyll, Std., P. O. Box 405, Media, PA 19063, 215-565-5242. Rental apartments in Europe.

Cruises

▲ **Celebrity Cruises**—5200 Blue Lagoon Drive, Miami, FL 33126, 305-262-8322, 800-437-3111. Also discount cruises for Royal Caribbean Cruise Lines.

▲ **Premier Cruise Lines**—P.O. Box 573, Cape Canaveral, FL 32920, 407-783-5061, 800-327-7113. Cruise the Bahamas, Nassau, Disney packages.

▲ **South Florida Cruises**—3561 NW 53 Court, Ft. Lauderdale, FL 33309, 305-739-7447, 800-327-7447. They buy group allotments on most cruise lines and pass the savings to you.

Airlines

▲ **American Airlines**—800-433-7300. Call for information regarding various travel options with the best rates. They have coupon books for senior travelers (62 years old).

▲ **Continental**—800-441-1135, 800-248-8996. Request any discounts when you make reservations. Senior citizens should inquire about Freedom Passport and Freedom Trips discounts.

▲ **Delta**—800-221-1212. Request any discounts when you make reservations. For those passengers 62 + , ask about the "Young at Heart" tickets.

▲ **Northwest**—800-225-2525. Request any discounts when you make reservations. For those passengers 62 + , ask about the Ultra fare rates.

▲ **TWA**—800-221-2000. Request any discounts when you make reservations. For those passengers 62 + , ask about the Senior Travel Pak rates.

▲ **United**—800-628-2868. Request any discounts when you make reservations. For those passengers 62 + , ask about the Silver Wings Plus rates.

▲ **U.S. Air**—800-428-4322. Request any discounts when you make reservations. For those passengers 62 + , ask about the Golden Opportunities coupon books.

Foreign Airlines

Contact each of these and ask for any special rates. If you are a senior citizen, be sure to ask for any programs for this age group.

▲ **Air Canada**—800-776-3000

▲ **British Airways**—800-247-9297

▲ **El Al**—800-223-6700, 212-768-9200

▲ **KLM Royal Dutch Airlines**—800-777-5553

▲ **Mexicana**—800-531-7921

▲ **SAS**—800-221-2350

▲ **Tap Air Portugal**—800-221-7370

Trains

Contact each of these and ask for any special rates. If you are a senior citizen, be sure to ask for any programs for this age group.

▲ **Amtrak**—800-872-7245

▲ **Austrian Federal Railways**—212-944-6880

▲ **British Tourist Office**—212-581-4700, 800-677-8585

▲ **German Rail**—800-308-3100

▲ **Greek National Tourists Org.**—212-421-5777

▲ **Irish Tourist Board**—800-223-6470

▲ **Italian State Railways**—212-397-2667

▲ **Luxembourg National Tourist Office**—
212-370-9850

▲ **Ontario, Canada, Northland**—800-268-9281

▲ **Portuguese National Tourist Office**—212-354-4403

▲ **Scandinavian National Tourist Office**—
212-949-2333

▲ **Via Rail Canada**—800-387-1144

Buses

Contact each of these and ask for any special rates. If you are a senior citizen, be sure to ask for any programs for this age group.

▲ **Gray Lines**—Check your local phone directory's yellow pages to assist you with the phone number in your locale.

▲ **Greyhound/Trailways**—Check your local phone directory's yellow pages to assist you with the phone number in your locale.

Car Rentals

Contact each of these and ask for any special rates. If you are a senior citizen, be sure to ask for any programs for this age group.

▲ **Alamo**—800-327-9633

▲ **Avis**—800-331-1212

▲ **Dollar**—800-800-4000

▲ **Hertz**—800-654-3131

▲ **National**—800-CAR-RENT

▲ **Thrifty Rent-A-Car**—800-367-2277

Hotels

Contact each of these and ask for any special rates. If you are a senior citizen, be sure to ask for any programs for this age group.

▲ **Best Western**—800-528-1234;
Hearing-impaired: 800-528-2222.

▲ **Choice Hotel International**,
Sleep Inn, Comfort, Quality, Clarion, Friendship Inn,
EconoLodge, Rodeway Inn—800-221-2222;
Hearing-impaired:
800-228-3323.

▲ **Days Inn**—800-247-5152;
Hearing-impaired: 800-222-3297

▲ **Doubletree Hotels**—800-528-0444

▲ **Hampton Inns**—800-HAMPTON

▲ **Hilton Hotels**—800-492-3232

▲ **Holiday Inns**—800-336-6330

▲ **Howard Johnson**—800-634-3464

▲ **Hyatt Hotels**—800-233-1234

▲ **La Quinta Motor Inn**—800-531-5900

▲ **Omni Hotels**—800-THE OMNI

▲ **Radisson Hotels**—800-333-3333

▲ **Ramada International**—800-228-9898

▲ **Red Lion Hotels**—800-547-8010

▲ **Rodeway Inns**—800-424-6423

▲ **Sheraton Hotels**—800-325-3535

▲ **Shoney's Inns**—800-222-2222

▲ **Stouffer Hotels**—800-468-3571

▲ **Travelodge**—800-255-3050

▲ **Vagabond Inns**—800-522-1555

▲ **Westin Hotels**—800-228-3000

Time is money; money is time. The more you have of the one, the less you need of the other. Travel is a wonderful way to break your routine, develop a new perspective on life, gain a better sense of personal history, and strengthen your hobby if you like to play tennis, golf, paint, collect antiques, etc. It's even more fun when you can save money in the process.

$ Cheaper Can Be Better $

O ne of the Barnes' Mottos is: "**Cheaper can be better**." Madison Avenue has tried to brainwash us into thinking if it doesn't have the right insignia or trade name it isn't worthy of purchasing. For everyday clothes, general foods, and household appliances, a few minutes in shopping can give you a great deal of savings.

Emilie's mother used to say, "You only get what you pay for." Since she was in the clothing business, she knew good fabrics by the very touch of the cloth between her fingers. However, there are times when you can buy high-quality goods at truly low prices.

There are many examples which prove the adage "Cheaper can be better."

Clothing Better for Less

▲ Co-op with other parents and swap baby clothes. Save those clothes in storage in boxes marked "1st Year," "2nd Year," "3rd Year," etc. When one of your younger children reach that age or a friend has a need for those clothes, you have a ready supply. What a bargain! Many of these are great for everyday wear, and if you're lucky you might even get some "special wear" clothes.

▲ Look for "recycled clothing" stores. Particularly in larger cities there are stores which take on consignment second-hand items which have only been worn once or twice. Emilie and I love to go into Pasadena and look through these clothing stores. You would be amazed at the fashions and bargains!

▲ Wait for sales in your favorite department store.

▲ Locate a factory outlet near your home in which to shop. Sometimes you have to drive an hour or more to shop, but the savings are worth the drive. Bunch up your desired purchases so you can buy several items at a time. Also let your friends and family know that you are going. See if they need anything while you are there. (They may even want to go with you.)

▲ Let your friends, relatives, and business associates know that you would be interested in buying or trading for some of their clothes when they get tired of them. Our son, Brad, gives most of his older clothes to a high school principal in our area. Tom just loves to get Brad's clothes, since they are usually like new. I have several friends who love to purchase my clothes. They are a perfect fit and style and the price is right. Look and talk around. There are a lot of bargains in someone's closet.

▲ In larger cities many manufacturers have "second" outlets which give tremendous savings to the public. Examine carefully the item to make sure you can accept the flaw. Many times the flaw won't show, or else an inexpensive designer patch can go over the spot and give an added flair to the garment.

▲ In Southern California are several stores which purchase from leading manufacturers' seconds, overruns, and year-end styles—which they discount at great savings. These are great sources for clothing.

▲ Take advantage of garage sales for good play clothes. We have found some excellent buys. In some cases the items have never been worn. (Yes, even the price tag is still attached!)

Eating Better for Less

▲ Look behind newly marked, higher-priced items at the front of a shelf. You may find a few of the items still marked at the old price. (However, many of the new cash registers have taken away this possibility. Still, it doesn't hurt to look.)

▲ Fruits and vegetables grown by local farmers tend to be fresher and more nourishing than those shipped from afar. My own garden is the best and cheapest of all. It provides us all year round with wonderful fruits, vegetables, and flowers.

▲ Canned light tuna is preferable for heavy recipes to the more costly solid white; it's less dry and has a richer flavor.

▲ For stews, pot roasts, and other dishes that are cooked a long time, cheaper cuts of meat (such as chuck) tend to be more moist and flavorful. Emilie highly recommends at her seminars the purchase of a Crockpot for your kitchen. Start cooking your meal in the morning, and at dinnertime it's ready for you to sit down and enjoy. Just add a salad and some French bread and your meal will be complete. When buying a Crockpot, choose one in which the pot can be lifted out for ease of cleaning. (Don't get the type that requires the pot to be cleaned together with the heating elements.)

▲ Try not to take your children shopping with you. They will put pressure on you to buy TV items, and your food costs will be higher. (As the children enter their teens, valuable teaching can take place at the supermarket. But it's not a good idea when they are young.)

▲ Don't assume that items at the end of aisles that are eye-catching are the cheapest or on sale. Look on lower shelves for other selections. Many times generic or other brands have good cost value.

▲ Get in the habit of using coupons. Be selective in buying only items you normally use. (However, venture out occasionally for an item you don't normally purchase. You might like your new brand better, and hopefully it will cost less.)

▲ Bruised, overripe bananas from the bargain bin add a much stronger flavor to banana breads, muffins, ice cream, and fruit puree than firm, perfect fruit.

▲ Many frozen vegetables, such as green peas and green beans, are better and more nourishing than fresh ones because they're frozen within hours of picking.

▲ Choose whole-grain breads and cereals rather than refined ones. You'll get more fiber as well as B vitamins and minerals (try the day-old bin).

▲ Potatoes boiled or baked whole in their skins retain nearly all their vitamins and minerals. Halving or peeling causes nutrient loss.

▲ Change your meal pattern. Instead of the same old routine—meats, potatoes, and vegetables for dinner every day—serve a hearty soup, an unusual casserole, or a main dish salad. Again, you might be interested in some of Emilie's cookbooks which are self-published. (Please write to us for more information. Our address is at the end of the book.)

▲ Buy plain, unsweetened cereals and add sliced fruit, raisins, and/or nuts instead of sugar.

▲ Take a hand calculator with you when you shop. Then you can break down the cost for true cost comparisons.

▲ Shop from a preselected list of foods from your menu planner. Through some preplanning of meals you can save $15 to $20 per week. Don't buy compulsively. Use discipline.

▲ Get in and out of the market as quickly as possible. The longer you stay the more you will spend.

▲ Don't go food shopping when you are hungry. You will purchase more when you are hungry.

▲ Pasta sauces made entirely of tomatoes and other vegetables have less fat and fewer calories than meaty ones, so add chicken or turkey at home. These meats have less fat, are less expensive, and are more nutritious for your family.

▲ Get day-old pastries and breads. I just love this bargain table in the market. You usually save 50 percent on these items. They are also good for making stuffing, French toast, and bread puddings.

▲ Ground chuck makes juicier, tastier hamburgers than ground round or ground sirloin. (You might be interested in Emilie's cookbooks that give you some healthier meat alternatives in your meal planning.)

$ Money-Saving Tips $
on Energy

Plans fail for lack of counsel, but with many advisers they succeed.

—Proverbs 15:22 NIV

As wise managers of your home, you want to look at ways you can be more cost-efficient. You might be amazed at how much money is wasted each month because of lack of discipline within your family. Energy is one topic which takes the whole family's cooperation to be effective. Get everyone in the act. Give incentives, rewards, and profit-sharing rebates if the whole family can reduce energy costs in the home. Keep a log of your utility costs and compare monthly as well as quarterly. Set a goal, and if it is met reward the family with something special.

We start with each month's utility bills to see if they are about normal. If below normal, we always beam with a smile to each other. But if it they are larger than normal we begin to ask some basic questions:

▲ Why is this item out of line? Change in seasons, fluctuation of temperature, lack of rain, or change in rates? We might even have a faulty appliance or a water or gas leak. Or maybe we are just leaving lights on longer than normal.

▲ Was there an error in reading the meter? Call the utility company and ask for a re-read. The rate per usage could be wrong. The unit multiplication could be wrong, which would give an error in calculation.

▲ How can we reduce our energy costs? Maybe we need to be more careful in our use of these appliances. Emilie and I used to get the whole family involved. This makes a great topic for our "Family Conference Time."

We spend needless money on heating and electric bills because we don't know what the best ways are to run our home and appliances. Here are some exciting tips to help you save lots of money by being aware of things we can do to help cut down on those high utility bills.

Humidifiers

Moist air retains heat. By investing in a humidifier or perhaps adapting your present heating system to include a humidifier, you can lower your thermostat by 2 to 4 degrees, which means a savings of 4 to 12 percent on your total heating bill. So in less than five years you will pay for your investment.

Drippy Water

Do you realize that just one drop of water per second leaking from a faucet can waste 60 gallons of water per week? Washing your hands can use 2 gallons of hot water. A five-minute shower takes about 20 gallons. And the average dishwasher uses 12 to 14 gallons of hot water per load. Air-drying the dishes can save up to 10 percent of the operating costs.

You may want to check your hot water heater. Did you know that for every 20 degrees the heater can be lowered you can cut the cost by 25 percent, and if you insulate your heater you can save another 15 percent?

▲ Take showers instead of baths (believe it or not, showers take less water than baths). A short shower uses 4 to 8 gallons where a bath uses 20 gallons or more.

▲ If you have a dishwasher, turn it off before the cycle ends and let the dishes air-dry.

▲ Keep your refrigerator defrosted regularly; clean those condenser coils on the back and bottom two times a year.

▲ Keeping your drapes and blinds closed, especially when you're not at home, will keep your home warmer in the winter and cooler in the summer.

▲ Locking your windows will give a tighter seal and help keep outside air out of your home.

▲ Fill your swimming pool with rainwater. Attach an elbow connection to your house's gutter spout and run a pipe from the elbow connection to your pool.

▲ Prevent sediments from building up in your water heater by draining it periodically.

▲ Any rooms that are not being used need not be heated. So close the doors and vents (guest rooms, extra baths, closets, etc). This will help lower heating bills.

▲ Insulation in the attic is probably the best way to reduce heat loss and air-conditioning loss—a very important and effective way to save on that utility bill!

▲ Use an insulated blanket for your water heater.

▲ Use cold water rather than hot water when washing your garments. Many modern fabrics and soaps are actually designed for cold-water washing.

▲ A moderate temperature setting on your water heater increases an appliance's efficiency, since the "normal" setting (usually about 140 degrees) supplies all the heat most families need.

▲ If your hot-water lines are some distance from your water heater you may want to wrap them with insulation.

▲ Add a "water-saver" adapter in each of your shower heads. This will drastically save on water consumption.

Heating Systems

▲ If you have a gas-fired heating system, have it professionally cleaned and serviced at least once a year. Oil-fired systems should be cleaned and serviced at least two times a year.

▲ For any heating system (forced air, hot water, steam, electric), keep radiators, air registers, and ducts clean, clear of dirt and debris, and free of obstructions (such as furniture and drapes).

▲ Some families install an electronic ignition. This does away with the need for a continuously burning pilot light and increases your savings substantially.

▲ You can save on heating costs by dressing to retain body heat. Layer extra clothes, so that as the day warms up you can remove them if you become too warm.

▲ A simple thing like keeping your windows sparkling clean in winter can help warm your home. Spotless window glass lets in more sunlight than grimy panes.

▲ To maintain your home's temperature, latch the windows instead of merely closing them. This gives a tighter seal.

▲ Install dual-glazed windows when building a new home or remodeling an older home. This can result in a savings of 8 to 10 percent on your utility bills.

▲ Make sure the damper in your fireplace is closed when it isn't being used. An open chimney allows a lot of valuable heat to escape.

▲ Remove window screens before winter arrives because fine-mist screen can reduce the amount of warming sunlight entering your home by up to 20 percent.

▲ Hot bathwater will help keep your bathroom warm in cold-weather months if you allow it to cool down before draining the tub. The water will add humidity that will also contribute to your home's comfort.

▲ Install a day/night thermostat in your home so you can better control your temperature when you need to. It will turn your furnace on in the morning before you get up, and it will turn it off whenever you so direct. If you are a working family, you need not keep the heating/cooling on all day. Before you arrive home the thermostat will turn the furnace on so the house will be comfortable when you arrive. Just like magic you can set all your needs with this type of thermostat.

▲ Periodically change the filters in the return air grill. A furnace with a dirty filter will cost more to operate.

Lights

Did you know that it's cheaper to turn a light on and off when entering and leaving a room than to just leave it on? Also, your light bulbs will last longer.

I have several lamps around our home which have timers. (Timers can be purchased in most hardware stores.) They will turn your lights on and off automatically. The savings could add up to 25 percent of your yearly electric bill. Also, it gives strangers the impression that someone is home while you are away from home.

Fluorescent lights use less electricity than incandescent light bulbs. They also illuminate more efficiently than bulbs. A 40-watt fluorescent tube gives more light than a 100-watt incandescent bulb while using less than half the current.

You may want to begin a "lights out" program or policy in your home with the family.

Dimmer switches can be purchased at most hardware stores and are very easily installed. These can increase your light bulb life up to 12 times while at the same time reducing your electricity usage.

Here are some more money-saving ideas.

- ▲ Rearrange your rooms. Let one properly shaded light do the work of three or four. If you're redecorating, use light colors. Dark colors absorb more light.

- ▲ Use lower-watt bulbs. Use three-way bulbs if possible. They let you adjust lighting intensity for your needs.

- ▲ Turn off all outdoor lights, except those necessary for safety and security.

- ▲ If you install bright security lights, consider controlling them with a photoelectric cell or timer that turns the lights on at dusk and off at dawn so you can avoid burning the lights unnecessarily. Fairly new on the market are floodlights which are activated by motion. These are great to illuminate certain areas when a family member comes home after dark. They go on only when there is motion, then turn off shortly afterward. This type of light is excellent for home security.

- ▲ To monitor lights in remote areas of the house, another possibility is to install a switch with a red pilot indicator on it. When the red light glows, you'll know that lights in those areas have been left on. These remote switches are available at hardware stores.

▲ Make sure that bulbs in remote places (attic, basement, garage, closets) haven't been left burning. Install automatic switches that shut off lights in a room when the door is closed.

▲ It's better to use one large bulb than several smaller ones. It requires six 25-watt bulbs to produce the light of a single 100-watt bulb.

▲ It's important that light fixtures be kept clean, because a dusty or dirty light fixture will absorb light. A dirty fixture will cause family members to turn on additional lights.

Take serious inventory of your energy costs. Particularly when you are on a fixed budget, you can acquire additional money for other needs in your home. The area of the country you live in will determine the potential for savings in lighting costs.

We all need to be aware of good and dependable stewardship of our natural resources. God intended for us to be good managers of the things He has given us to enjoy in this world. It makes sense for all of us to conserve our energy use and not to waste these precious resources.

Energy waste costs money, and money comes from work. How much work do you want to save on utility bills?

$ **Retail at the Grass Roots** $

E veryone knows how to run a yard sale/garage
sale: Just clean out your garage and home, pile
all your unwanted junk in the front yard, stand up an umbrella, pull
up a lawn chair, and wait for the customers to come with all their
cash.

Wrong!

Your little retail business is in competition with the other businesses in the area, even including the regular retailing stores.

You've got to attract your would-be customers to your sale and
hope that they will buy. In Southern California most of the year is a
great time for such an adventure. Here are some tips that we use to
maximize our efforts.

Planning

▲ Check your local ordinances on yard sales. If you live in a
gated community or condominium with a homeowner's association, be sure to check the regulations.

▲ Research other yard sales to see what's selling and how the
people are displaying products and advertising the sale.

▲ Consider getting the whole neighborhood together for a sale.
Buyers like big, active sales. (It's also a great way to get to
know your neighbors.) If you live in a cul-de-sac, you can
block off the traffic and set up a walking yard sale. Customers love the added adventure.

▲ Have each homeowner set up, price, sell, and be responsible
for his or her own sales. If you pool everything together, be

sure the items are priced in writing and the owners' names clearly marked so you can easily keep track of the sales.

▲ Keep track of the sales yourself. You can add merchandise to the sale by asking neighbors if they would like to sell items at your sale on consignment. If the contributor does not work at the sale, a seller's commission of 35 to 50 percent is fair.

▲ Stock a change box or pockets of your apron with at least 50 singles, a few fives, and 20 dollars in quarters, dimes, and nickels. Price items so you won't have to use pennies. If you accept checks, ask for identification and note driver's license, credit card numbers, and car license too. I usually recommend not to accept checks unless you know the people. (This saves a lot of problems in trying to collect on a bad check.)

▲ If your neighbors are not participating, let them know of your sale. They may want to shop early or put "no parking" signs in front of their houses.

Timing

▲ Saturday morning is the best time. If you have a lot of merchandise, you might consider a two-day event, but usually Saturday is sufficient. Customers will come early, so you need to be ready. Don't wait until the last minute. Many early birds will want to shop before the advertised beginning. Decide beforehand what your policy will be.

▲ Avoid holiday weekends when buyers may be out of town.

Advertising

▲ Put a classified ad in free shopping guides and a newspaper a day or two in advance and on the day of the sale. Experienced yard sellers like to run ads on the same days that good advertising and coupons appear.

▲ In the ad, include the location (with cross street), dates, opening and closing hours, and a few appealing items and prices. Telephone number is optional (this information creates a need for someone to be available to answer specific questions).

▲ Post 3x5 index cards on bulletin boards in churches, supermarkets, and Laundromats. Include the same information as in the ad.

▲ Make big, readable signs or buy them at the hardware store. Red letters on a white background are good. Be sure the letters are big enough to be read by people driving by.

▲ Post the signs on your own property or get permission to put them on neighbors' properties. Place signs drawing attention to your sale around entrances to streets leading to your home. BE SURE TO TAKE THEM DOWN PROMPTLY AFTER THE SALE.

▲ Jazz up your sale with balloons, a child in a clown suit, or a 20-foot banner made with a computer. Funny signs also attract attention.

Supplies

▲ An electric outlet to plug in TV's, power tools, and blenders to show that they work.

▲ Tape measure and yardsticks.

▲ Boxes, bags, string, and cord for securing items to the buyer's car.

▲ Plastic covers if rain or snow is forecast.

Merchandise

▲ The more merchandise, color, and variety you've got, the bigger the crowd you'll draw. That's why "block sales" are so good. You want to stop traffic and get people out of their cars.

▲ If you are short of merchandise, you might want to augment your sale by going to auctions, yard sales, swap meets, thrift stores, and moving sales.

▲ Clean, new-looking items sell faster and for more money. Wash the dishes. Wash and iron the clothes. Dust, clean, and polish the furniture. Take a few minutes to clean your toaster oven and you can double your price. Eye appeal is very important.

▲ It's a good idea to oil garden implements.

▲ If the item doesn't work, mark it "as is." Some do-it-yourself repair person wants your old appliances, especially TV's, for the parts.

▲ Buyers like high-ticket items such as power tools and exercise equipment because they're a good deal. Tools are popular—hand tools, garden tools, and power tools such as sabre saws, drills, and electric sanders. Shoppers also like all types of exercise equipment—rowing machines, Stair Masters, exercise bicycles, and weight stations. Toolboxes sell well, and so do bicycles.

▲ People will purchase typewriters, but they usually shy away from computers.

▲ Secondhand clothes sell, but they've got to look good. A pile of wrinkled clothes can only be sold as rags.

▲ Shoppers will buy bed linen if it's clean, pressed, and folded nicely. You might even put plastic around it for a near-new look. Comforters sell well.

▲ Many buyers are suspicious of baby cribs, infant toys, and clothes because of hygiene.

▲ Wood furniture sells better than upholstered.

▲ Puzzles and board games don't sell well because buyers suspect that pieces are missing. Put parts into plastic bags and make sure all the pieces are there.

▲ A "free box" for adults or children may increase goodwill and sales.

Pricing

▲ Base prices on what others will pay, not entirely on what an item is worth to you. Things you consider worthless junk may be valuable additions to someone's collection of comic books, dolls, baseball cards, etc.

▲ If you do sell something for less than the posted price, try not to let other customers overhear it because they'll want to pay less too. We were at a recent yard sale with a sign that read "Make an offer on all prices." Some people just love to negotiate prices.

▲ Inability to haggle can mean you'll make less money or you'll be left with a lot of goods.

▲ Cooking utensils sell very well and can be priced a little higher than other items.

▲ You can start high and reduce your price, but once a customer sees a price tag, you can't raise it. However, you can change prices between customers.

▲ Twenty to 39 percent of current retail selling price is a good rule of thumb for everything but collectibles and used clothing. Look in catalogs from Sears or Montgomery Ward to help you on pricing. Shop the neighborhood yard sales a few weeks ahead of time to see what particular items are selling for.

▲ Adult used clothing sells for about 10 percent of retail. Vintage items sell for much more.

▲ If certain items are selling too quickly, you probably have them priced too low. Raise the prices on the remaining items.

▲ If your objective is to get rid of your merchandise, price items on the low side.

▲ If you don't want to dicker with customers, put fair prices on the tags. If an interested buyer seems to think the item is priced too high, drop it on the spot or arrange to call him or her later if the item doesn't sell.

Display

▲ Arrange colorful items for eye appeal.

▲ A jumble of items looks like a bargain, so neatness doesn't always count.

▲ Set up the day before. Don't wait until the last minute. As day breaks, pull out your tables with merchandise on them. Make sure that all items are priced.

▲ Keep merchandise off the ground or sidewalks. This way the shoppers are more likely to buy and less likely to trip. Sheets of plywood over trash cans make wonderful tables, along with picnic and card tables. Cover the tables with clean sheets.

▲ Arrange tables in a horseshoe or V shape facing the street so that people driving by can see the full assortment. Keep the view open; don't park personal cars in the front of the house.

▲ Display your large items up front so they have a lot of eye appeal. Have balloons attached to draw attention.

▲ Some people recommend arranging like items together, while others separate men, women, and children items. Others contend that it's best to intermix everything.

▲ Put clothes on hangers and hang them on bars, trees, or from the garage door tension rods. Make them easy to examine.

▲ Furniture should be arranged in attractive groupings. Provide room between the items so the shoppers can easily inspect.

▲ Have one table just for jewelry. A black background gives added sparkle to the display.

After the Sale

▲ Clean up thoroughly afterward, and be sure to take down all signs. You want to keep happy neighbors.

▲ Reward the family by doing something different—a dinner out, a barbecue, a roller skating party, a trip to the yogurt shop. We've even had a block party to celebrate a good day of sales.

▲ Call the Salvation Army, Goodwill, church, or home for the blind to come and pick up all leftovers.

Advice for Shoppers

▲ Hit the sales early the first day. If you see a good sale and want to stock an upcoming one of your own, consider a buyout of the whole sale.

▲ Look for good buys on large appliances and furniture at moving sales. Sellers who are moving are more willing to bargain because they need to unload merchandise quickly.

▲ Don't be afraid to bargain for a better price.

▲ Take a measuring tape to make sure items will fit in the space you have allotted for them at home or office.

$ Great Fund-Raising Ideas $

Many of us are members of churches, clubs, fraternities, or sororities that are looking for ways to raise funds. About the time we realize there is a need to raise funds, we scratch our heads to think of creative ways to supplement our budget. Our minds go blank! Some of these ideas from our readers can provide real help.

Service, time, and talent auction. In this auction you don't sell material possessions but pledges for service, time, and talent. Items you might include: babysitting, a resort area condominium, home-baked cookies once a month for a year, car service to and from the airport for a future plane trip. Each donation is the generous giving of self.

Cleanup crew. A great high school or teenage project is to take the place of professional street cleaners when you need to clean the streets of the fall leaves. Charge the neighbors or business tenants a fair wage. It doesn't take many students to earn a fair amount of money for their special project.

Hill of beans. Here's a fund-raiser based on a hill of beans—kidneys, pintos, lentils, split peas, limas, and more. Members of your club can donate these beans. Combine them into a colorful, flavorful mix, then bag them in plastic bags of two cups each and sell them for $2 each along with instructions for rinsing, soaking, and making soup. Tie a colorful ribbon at the top of your bag to provide colorful eye appeal.

Lip sync. Hold a lip-sync show. While a recording of a real singer plays, each child performs one or two songs, imitating the artists' style and mouthing the lyrics. Have rehearsals so the students can pool the songs, tapes, records, and lyrics. You can even make costumes with materials on hand and such finishing touches as feathers or jewelry. Sell tickets or take a freewill offering.

Krazy kalendar. For your special fund-raiser make up a unique calendar showing particular days of the month with specified amounts of money to put away for this fund-raising idea. In a typical week in July ask for 50 cents on Sunday "if you didn't go to church tonight," followed by "1 cent for each year of your age above 21" on Monday; "10 cents if you have a patio or deck" on Tuesday; "25 cents if you turned on the air conditioner" on Wednesday; "5 cents for each glass of water you drank" on Thursday; "1 cent for each page of a book you read" on Friday; and "10 cents if you drank lemonade" on Saturday. Deposit the money in a jar and contribute jointly for your special fund-raiser.

House numbers. Raise extra money by painting street numbers on the curbs of your neighborhood streets. Be sure to clear the idea with your local police department. Call on the neighbors to presell the orders. Depending on the economic level of your neighborhood, a fair price would be in the $3 to $5 range. Stencil black numbers in 6x10-inch white rectangles on curbs, steps, and sidewalks. You might even have local merchants donate the paint. You will find the police and fire departments delighted with the easy-to-read addresses.

Tasting bee. If you are passing up the usual barbecues, fish fries, pancake breakfasts, etc. you might want to try something different to make money—a "May Tasting Bee." At theme tables decorated with flowers, flags, and costumed dolls representing various parts of the world you can serve portions of a variety of American, European, Mexican, and Oriental foods. For a fixed price you can sample food from as many tables as you wish. The dessert table could be an extra cost if you wish. The only eating utensils needed are teaspoons and toothpicks. You could also preprint the food recipes and sell them for a nominal cost.

Twenty talents. Give your group of 20 youngsters $1 each to purchase supplies for a craft or baking project. You can also pool your money for larger projects. You can even contribute a little extra money on your own if you like. You can also use materials found around the home. In three or four weeks you can bring the crafts or baked goods to a central area in which they can be sold. You can turn the original $20 into much more by selling or auctioning off cookies, cakes, holiday decorations, aprons, stuffed toys, baby quilts, or covered photograph albums.

Seesaw marathon. Schedule a seesaw contest within your group and seesaw from a Friday afternoon until Sunday afternoon. You can presell pledges from your neighbors, friends, and family based on the number of hours the students keep going. The students can teeter-totter in three-hour shifts.

Use your own creative imagination in creating your fund-raising projects. These efforts bring out the organizational ability of the various members, and seem to bring the members closer together. Those who participate in these projects also become more familiar in the sponsoring group's purposes.

**Start a Home Business
in the '90s**

*I will trust and not be afraid, for the Lord God is my
strength and song, and He has become my salvation.*

—Isaiah 12:2

Since 85 percent of new businesses are started
by women in their homes, Emilie personally
wanted to address this subject.

▲ ▲ ▲

Today's woman approaches the 1990s with much excitement.
We've come a long way, women: The '80s found us making a lot of
changes from home to work—stress, frustration, disorganization,
and fatigue. Our priorities went out the window along with our
organized homes and meals. We gave up our children to sitters and
daycare and our meals to fast-food stores. Our spiritual life moved
into low gear.

However, new changes are coming into focus. We are tired of the
tired '80s. More women are feeling the desire to be at-home
mothers and career women. We will see working women find balance between work and home and new interests in home business.

My mother became a single working parent when my father died.
(I was 11 years old.) She opened a small dress shop and we lived in
the back in a small three-room apartment. Home and career were
mixed. Mom not only sold clothing but worked late into the night

doing alterations. (Bookwork was done after-hours.) We survived because we all helped in a time of need and survival.

When our children were small I developed a small business out of our home; the extra money was for extra things. I was able to do that because I felt somewhat organized and in control of our home.

This may be the year that God will bring into *your* life the desire to be an at-home woman and to develop a from-home business. Of course, to be successful it does take time, creativity, balance, and desire. Our ministry, **More Hours In My Day**, began out of our home and has stayed there for over 11 years. Books have been written, seminars given, and mail orders sent from our door to many of yours.

Our typist, Sheri, has a typing service from her home and is enjoying better profits than ever before. A dear and longtime friend, Rose, has a small business called "Tiffany Touch," in which she goes into other people's homes in her area and does anything they need done, from organizing a drawer to hanging pictures. A mother with a new baby designed a slip over the head bib that is sold all over the country out of her home. Still another mom created designer baby bottles—she changed baby needs into cash of over 1 million dollars!

Connie Lund, out of Olympia, Washington, created a small devotional flip chart of inspiration called "Reaching Up to God." Through its sales she is sending her daughter through college. When her daughter comes home for vacations she helps collate and tie. Most at-home businesses develop family oneness, with all members working together to help with the business.

Direct sales are popular and profitable: Tupperware, Avon, Shaklee, Amway, Mary Kay, Home Interiors, "Christmas Around the World," Successful Living Books, Choice Books. From home parties to door-to-door, these are just a few examples.

One woman I read about shops for working women, buying groceries and gifts and running errands from dry cleaning to stamps at the post office. She even delivered a lunch to a school child who forgot it at home.

Another creative mom does gift wrapping for people (especially men in offices) that led to food baskets and then homemade wreaths and floral arrangements.

Another mom advertised her famous chili recipe for $1—and sold enough to buy Christmas presents for the whole family. She was very pleased and surprised. Amiee makes colorful earrings. Women saw them on her and wanted a pair for themselves. From friends to boutique shops, sales multiplied.

All kinds of arts and crafts have created many added funds to the family income.

I was visiting some friends who received an adorable loaf of bread shaped like a teddy bear. This novelty gift is now being shipped all over the state.

Nancy is a single parent who quit her computer job and started her own service in her home. She is now home with her three children and still runs a very successful business.

Nancy and Elizabeth teamed up to design and sell Christian greeting cards, business cards, and Christmas cards. They are doing very well.

Some women are working at home as an employee—sales rep, technical service rep, claim adjuster. Many others are salaried employees but spend most of their time in the field. Their employers typically don't provide an office, so their files, desk phones, etc. are in their homes. Many can do part-time employment in the same way. (You do have to ask yourself whether you have the space in your home for this type of employment.)

I have a friend who reps designer clothing out of her home four times a year. She sends out invitations with days and hours, then books appointments and helps the women coordinate their wardrobes.

As we move into the 1990s, set your desires high and chart out your goals for your future. Where would you like to be next year at this time? What will you need to accomplish to be there?

When can you start? Possibly now. 1. Your desire is to be working from home—by next year. 2. Make calls and talk with friends, family, and business associates. 3. Perhaps you need to take a class on business, sales, design, etc.

Many of you may be happy just where you are. Others may want to cut hours to be at home a little more. What do you want to accomplish in the 1990s? Start with a positive attitude, strong desire, and creativity wrapped with prayer.

My desire is to see the busy woman get back to traditional values and to use her God-given creativity wherever she may be in or out of the home.

Here are some ideas on how to begin a business at home.

Research

1. Find others who are in your same field of home business and talk with them. They can provide a wealth of information.

2. Will it benefit you to advertise in your local telephone book?

3. What kind of advertising should you use other than word of mouth?

Goals

1. Determine a time schedule to be at home with your business. Example: Within one year.

2. Sign up for a class at your local community college on simple business bookkeeping.

Finances

1. Draw up a projected budget for yourself. What will be your credits and your debits? How much money do you need to launch your business?

2. Consider the costs involved in advertising.

3. Set aside some money for start-up expenses and supplies, such as a typewriter, copy machine, furniture, and small desktop items, (stapler, scissors, etc.).

4. Start writing down hidden costs. There will always be expenses that you did not count on, so the more research you do the less likely you will have a lot of surprises.

Home Preparation

1. What area will you use and how much space do you need?

2. Can you use your existing phone system?

3. Do you need a desk, work tables, file cabinets, etc.?

4. Will any carpentry work be required?

Legalities

1. Get information on what legal matters need to be considered. Some home businesses require a business license. Check with your local county records department.

2. Obtain a resale number if needed.

3. What kind of deductions are you eligible for? Contact a CPA who is knowledgeable in the field of home business deductions.

Hours

1. Think through how many hours you can reasonably work per day, per week, per month.
2. Will you need to work around children's schedules?
3. Will you have regular business hours?
4. When will you clean your home, cook meals, etc.?
5. Don't forget *you*. Schedule time to do a few things for yourself: hair appointments, shopping, church, friends, Bible studies, etc.

As in many situations, your home business will involve a lot of trial and error. You'll learn much as you grow along, but the benefits will be great. An excellent book from one of our instructors, Donna Otto of Scottsdale, Arizona, is *The Stay-at-Home Mom* (Harvest House Publishers). It's a book that applauds the stay-at-home mom and cheers her on with practical ideas to make the journey an adventure. She has several chapters dealing with making and saving money at home. According to Donna, "Often it's the need for additional income that makes a mom take outside employment. Yet it's possible and practical to stay at home and generate income. You need conviction, discipline, and a plan."

Help!
I'm Being Audited!

Render to Caesar the things that are Caesar's, and to God the things that are God's.

—Matthew 22:21

Over the past 15 years we have been audited three times, and I cringe each time I receive an envelope from the IRS. My heart beats faster, I get nervous, the palms of my hands get moist, and it just ruins my day. However, after going through these three audits I have gained some valuable experience that might help you get ready for this occasion.

First you need to get rid of at least four myths that the average American has.

1. **The government is picking on me.** Your return was selected for audit for one of two reasons: Either someone has "turned you in" or a computer has found inconsistencies in your return. It's a matter of probabilities. If your return reveals deductions that, in the opinion of the IRS, exceed an acceptable percentage in a certain category, you may be selected for an audit.

2. **I must have done something wrong.** Most Americans are honest when filing tax returns. IRS audits usually show no evidence that the taxpayer deliberately tried to cheat the government. Most errors are mathematical or the taxpayer can't supply proof for the deduction.

3. **I'm going to be fined or receive a heavy penalty.** If the IRS interprets the regulation differently from you or your tax consultant, the penalty amounts to little more than a few dollars for back taxes plus interest.

4. **I'll get those guys/gals at the IRS.** This is not a good attitude. Treat them as professionals who specialize in tax laws. There is no need to place the auditor on the defensive. The emotions of a pending audit take you through anger, guilt, fear, and even revenge.

While an audit is not a pleasant way to spend a morning or afternoon, you can avoid some problems if you adhere to the following eight suggestions.

1. **Keep a positive attitude.** As you approach your audit, eliminate all the myths you have been exposed to. Be upbeat and confident that the deductions you have taken are within the legal limits allowed by our government. The law is on your side.

2. **Organize your materials.** If you have followed through with many of our organizational ideas in our various books, you will have your "perfect boxes" set up which store all your records, canceled checks, invoices, and receipts to support your claim that certain expenses should be considered legitimate deductions. Many times the auditor will judge the credibility of your report's accuracy by how you keep your records and how organized you are in supporting your deductions.

3. **Choose your tax preparer wisely.** If you use a "short form" return you can probably get by without the help of a tax professional. However, if you choose to take advantage of legitimate deductions, hire a qualified tax expert to prepare your return.

Because of the ever-changing tax laws, you want to make sure you select someone who knows the tax laws and is also experienced as a tax preparer. (A tax preparer is skilled at preparing forms, while a tax adviser knows the tax laws and can advise you on deductions to which you are entitled.)

Seek out personal recommendations from people you respect. Word of mouth is the best way to find this person. If you don't have that type of networking you may start by looking in the yellow pages. Be sure to interview the person to make sure you feel comfortable with your respective chemistries.

4. **Take your tax adviser to your audit.** Even though this will cost you money, you would be ill-advised to go alone. The person

who prepared your taxes is the most likely one to go with you. He or she is best trained to answer the auditor's questions. Some tax preparers recommend that you stay home while they represent you. Many times the presence of the taxpayer simply complicates matters. You must go only to give information when you are asked specifically. Don't volunteer information. Give only the facts.

5. Treat your auditor professionally. Assume that he or she is a professional and treat him with that dignity. Respect him as someone who is doing a thankless job. My experience is that he will be fair as long as you have respect for him and the system. If your return is done with fairness and truthfulness, with legitimate deductions, you will have a fairly pleasant experience. On the other hand, if you have been deceptive and inaccurate you will certainly not enjoy the experience.

6. Be confident of your position. There is no need to be intimidated by your auditor. You need not apologize for a deduction. If you are entitled to a deduction you should not hesitate to take it. The IRS not only *allows* you to take certain deductions but actually *encourages* you to do so. If you have a home business you might want to obtain "Tax Guide for Small Business" (publication #334). Call your local IRS office to obtain this publication.

7. Tell the truth. All the auditor is looking for is truthful verification of your return. He or she is trained to recognize a false receipt or a false statement. He is fairly tolerant of logical reasons for deductions, but he doesn't have much tolerance when he is lied to or deceived.

8. Be aware of appeal procedures. If you are not satisfied with the auditor's interpretation of the law, you can always appeal that decision. The auditor will be glad to familiarize you with this process.

Use this process as a positive learning experience for future tax reporting. You will gain a lot of insight throughout all this. The downside is that it will cost you money—win or lose. If you win, the cost will be having your tax preparer join you in the audit and the cost of losing time off from your work. If you lose, it will also cost you the amount of tax adjustment, any interest charges, and any penalty.

Go with the proper attitude and know that the law is with you.

$ How to Get Property Tax Bills Reduced $

One of the habits I have when we go out for dinner is to look over the bill before I pay. You would be amazed at how many errors I find on our bill. I would say that at least 50 percent of our bills have errors (which are usually overcharges).

Because of this habit, I look at all bills which come into our home. Because of the size of our real estate tax bills, I want to make sure they are right, so I spend some time making sure they are reasonable.

Your tax bill will usually state on it what the deadline for appeal is. If not, call the assessor's office to get that information.

Here are some ideas to help you review your yearly real estate tax bill:

Find out how your taxes are figured. Property tax bills are determined by multiplying part or all of your home's assessed value by a specific tax rate—for example, $5 per $100 of assessed value. Your local assessor determines that value.

If you aren't sure of the method that is used in your area, ask. A local real estate friend or the assessor's office can tell you the method used. The most common approaches include these four:

1. **The fractional method.** Your tax assessment is figured as a specific percentage of the home's full value. The assessor might figure your home's worth at $80,000, but the local tax ratio might be 50 percent. In that case the tax would be figured on $40,000. If the rate were $5 per $100 of assessed value, the bill would be $2000.

2. **The full-value method.** The tax rate is applied to 100 percent of the home's value. Usually the tax rate is lower and is proportional to the fractional method above.

3. **The construction-cost method.** Linked to how much it would cost to reconstruct that same home today.

4. **The comparable-sales method.** The assessment is based on the selling price of homes similar to yours in the same neighborhood.

Check the assessor's appraisal of your home. Legally you have the right to check records and worksheets dealing with your tax bill. When you audit these records, make sure to verify these items:

- ▲ Square footage
- ▲ Size of lot
- ▲ Correctly described building materials
- ▲ Proper school district, sanitation district, water district, etc.
- ▲ Check other homes in area that are similar in size to yours

- ▲ Number of rooms and baths
- ▲ Any outbuildings that no longer exist
- ▲ Accurate cost of improvements
- ▲ Right township
- ▲ Make sure home is properly located.

Make sure that the assessment ratio is correct. Mathematical mistakes are more likely to occur when your assessment is based on fractional versus full value rates. If your home is assessed higher than the rest of the homes in your neighborhood, you could compile your own assessment/sales ratio. Add up the recent sales prices of 12 or more homes in your tax district that are similar to yours, then look up the assessed value of those homes in the public tax records. Divide the total sales values by the total assessment to get an average assessment ratio. If this figure is substantially below the ratio used for your home, you have a good case for reevaluation of your property tax bill.

Make an informal appeal. When you can, show an obvious error. It is often possible to sit down with the assessor and get your bill reduced (and/or a refund from past overcharges) without having to go through a formal hearing before an appeal board.

Make a formal appeal. If you believe that a mistake has been made on your property taxes and the assessor does not voluntarily make the change for you, you probably have the right to make a formal protest. Check with your local office to see what procedures are necessary to file a formal appeal. When you have a set time, be sure you go to the appeal prepared. Bring:

- ▲ Photographs
- ▲ Facts you have gathered
- ▲ A professional appraisal of your home (this will cost you money to have done)

- ▲ Plans of your home
- ▲ Statements about property values from real estate experts

If you win, your tax bill will be reduced and you will receive a revised bill. If you lose, you may appeal to a higher court, depending upon your local laws. Yes, there is effort required, but the savings may be worth the effort.

$ How Much House $
Can You Afford?

The wise man saves for the future, but the foolish man spends whatever he gets.

—Proverbs 21:20

The great American dream is to own your own home. Yet that dream has become more and more difficult to achieve, depending upon what region of the country you live in.

Emilie and I remember our first house hunt. Those $20,000 homes were so beautiful, with a big yard, a two-car garage, built-in appliances, three bedrooms with a living room, and a den. When the salesman told us we didn't qualify, we were heartbroken. For several weeks we didn't continue our search for the American dream. Finally we did find a home in the $13,000 range, and we were on our way.

You might be asking "How much house can I afford?" The first thing you need to know when shopping for a home is how much you can reasonably spend. For most people this converts into "How large a mortgage can I afford?"

Lenders apply underwriting guidelines to each mortgage application. One of the most common tests is the debt-to-income ratio. This ratio compares levels of income with various debt expenses. Acceptable ratios are based on what a future homeowner can spend to successfully support a mortgage and also take care of other obligations.

As a general rule of thumb, one-third of your gross income may be spent on housing expenses, one-third on taxes, and the remaining third on your living expenses (see Chapter 13 for more information regarding this).

Lenders generally like to see that your monthly housing expenses do not exceed 28 to 30 percent of your monthly gross income, referred to as a "front-end ratio." Housing expenses include principal and interest payments on your mortgage, as well as real estate taxes, insurance, and any other applicable fees, such as condominium fees.

To calculate your monthly mortgage payment, refer to the Mortgage Payment Table below. Estimates of your real estate taxes, homeowner's insurance, and miscellaneous fees can be obtained from the seller of the home or your real estate agent.

The other debt-to-income ratio considered by lenders is your "back-end ratio." Typically, your housing expenses plus other monthly payments (such as auto loans, student loans, and credit card balances) should not exceed 36 percent of your gross income.

These are general guidelines. Acceptable ratios vary by lender, mortgage type, and your unique situation.

Monthly Payment Table

Equal Monthly Payments to Amortize a Loan of $1000

Rate (%)	15 Years	25 Years	30 Years
7	8.99	7.07	6.65
7½	9.27	7.39	6.99
8	9.56	7.72	7.34
8½	9.85	8.05	7.69
9	10.14	8.39	8.05
9½	10.44	8.74	8.41
10	10.75	9.09	8.78
10½	11.05	9.44	9.15
11	11.37	9.80	9.52
11½	11.68	10.16	9.90
12	12.00	10.53	10.29

To calculate your monthly payments:

$$\frac{\text{Loan amount}}{1000} \quad X \quad \begin{array}{c}\text{Payment factor from}\\ \text{above chart}\end{array}$$

For example, the monthly payment on a $100,000 15-year mortgage at an interest rate of $10\frac{1}{2}\%$ would be calculated as follows:

$$\frac{\$100,000}{1000} \quad X \quad 11.05 \quad = \quad \$1105 \text{ per month}$$

Think ahead of your near-future needs and then stretch your purchase level, because you will probably be improving your financial status in the next three to five years; however, don't get to the point where all your extra funds go to a house. Then you will become a slave to the house and won't have the funds to provide extras for the home and the necessary funds for God's opportunities for your life.

We know of many families in our area who have developed great family tensions because everything goes to pay for the mortgage. When that happens, you know you have leveraged your money too much.

Plan for the future, but don't let it make you a slave.

$ House-Hunting $
Checklist

My God shall supply all your needs according to His riches in glory.

—Philippians 4:19

Buying or renting a house, apartment, or condo can sometimes be a source of stress. By mid-summer, the anxiety of being settled before school starts can cause you to make the wrong decisions when house-hunting in a hurry.

This checklist can help you keep track of the special features of the homes you've seen. Use it to compare them and to single out that special house you want to make your home.

This organized shopping list can be kept and copies made. It will enable you to look back and compare.

If you have a Polaroid camera, take a picture of each home and attach it to the back of each checklist form.

This type of organization will certainly give you more credibility with the realtor and home-seller. They will both give you the benefit of being a wise buyer.

It's amazing how all apartments, condos, townhouses, and homes look the same after you have spent the weekend looking at various prospects. On the back of this form keep not only a picture, but also any notes that should be jotted down.

If time permits, drive past the schools, churches, shopping centers, malls, etc. The right neighborhood is worthy of all the information you can gather. You will probably be in this new residence for some time.

HOUSE-HUNT RECORD

Date_____

Address of home_____ Age_____

Best route to take_____

_____

Owner of Home_____ Phone #_____

Salesperson_____

House design_____

House color_____

No. of square feet_____ Size of lot_____

Asking price_____ Down payment $_____

Monthly payment $_____

Type of utilities_____ Cost per month $_____

Other costs_____

Garage? ☐ 1 Car ☐ 2 Car ☐ Larger ☐ Carport

Condition/type of roof_____

Living room: Size_____ Flooring_____

Kitchen: Size_____ Flooring_____

Dining room: Size_____ Flooring_____

Storage space: Adequate? ☐ Yes ☐ No

Bedrooms: Number_____ Sizes_____

Bathrooms: Number_____ Sizes_____ Colors_____

Fixtures and tile condition _____

Water pressure check_____

Family room: Size_____ Flooring_____

Foyer: Size_____ Closet space_____

Game room: Size_____ Flooring_____

Basement: Size_____ ☐ Finished ☐ Unfinished

Laundry room: Size_____ Flooring_____

Other_____

☐ Central Air ☐ Fireplace Location(s)_____

Overall interior condition_____

☐ Patio_____ ☐ Pool_____ ☐ Pantry_____

Distance from work: Miles_____ Time_____

Distance from shopping: Miles_____ Time_____

Neighborhood rating_____

Overall rating of home and property_____

Schools: Quality_____ Distance from home_____

Comments_____

Husband's first impression_____

Wife's first impression_____

$ Lowering Your $ Moving Costs

Fear not, for I am with you; be not dismayed, for I am your God. I will strengthen you, yes, I will help you; I will uphold you with My righteous right hand.

—Isaiah 41:10 NKJV

We are a country in transit; we move every four years. We move for various reasons: We can't take the weather anymore, our children relocate, we get a new job, we retire, we go to the Sunbelt.

In California our freeways are crowded with moving vans, some leaving, many coming. Interstate moving is very costly; the average is around $2500 but can go up considerably if you have a lot of furniture or a long move.

You can cut about 20 percent from your bill if you follow these ideas:

▲ Plan a garage or yard sale (see Chapter 52 for details).

▲ Move on a weekday. Fees can be 50 percent higher on weekends.

▲ Sell any cars, trucks, bicycles, and all-terrain vehicles that you aren't using or that aren't worth the expense of moving.

▲ Pack everything yourself. Most movers provide cartons and wrapping paper. Also, remove doors, unhook electrical appliances, and disassemble furniture. This can save you 10 to 15 percent of your moving costs.

▲ Don't keep movers waiting. This is at both ends of the move. Standby time will add to your bill.

▲ Have friends, relatives, and family help you on moving day. They can take many boxes out to the truck for their loading. Each trip is a money-saver for you.

▲ Get a binding estimate in writing. It may be higher than a nonbinding estimate, but the price is guaranteed. Usually the actual cost exceeds the estimate.

▲ Know your rights and responsibilities. If the movers damage your possessions or deliver them late, you may be entitled to a partial refund or reimbursement of actual replacement costs. There may be some items that you are responsible for. Make sure you know what they are.

There are so many details to remember before moving time, and often important things are forgotten until it's too late. Here is a checklist of the essential details that must be taken care of.

Transfer of Records

▲ School records
▲ Auto registration and driver's license
▲ Bank—savings and checking accounts
▲ Medical records from doctors and dentists
▲ Eyeglass prescription
▲ Pet immunization records
▲ Legal documents
▲ Church and other organizations
▲ Insurance

Services to Be Discontinued

▲ Telephone company
▲ Electric, gas, and water company
▲ Layaway purchases

▲ Cleaners—don't move without picking up all your clothes!

▲ Fuel company

▲ Milk delivery

▲ Newspaper delivery

▲ Cable television

▲ Pest control

▲ Water softener or bottled water

▲ Garbage service

▲ Diaper service

Change of Address

▲ Local post office

▲ Magazines

▲ Friends and relatives

▲ Insurance company

▲ Creditors and charge accounts

▲ Lawyer

▲ Church

Getting Ready

▲ Reserve a moving company if needed.

▲ Prepare to pack by enlisting some volunteers. Neighbors or friends from church are likely candidates and are usually very willing to help.

▲ Collect boxes from local supermarkets and drugstores. Be sure to go to stores early in the day, before the boxes are flattened and thrown out. Some moving companies will loan you boxes (such as wardrobe boxes).

▲ Buy felt marking pens to color-code your boxes: yellow for the kitchen; blue for bedroom #1; green for bedroom #2; orange for garage; violet for laundry room; etc.

▲ Prepare a work area (such as a card table) that can be used for wrapping and packing your goods.

▲ Clean and air the refrigerator and kitchen range.

▲ Be sure that gas appliances are properly disconnected.

▲ Make a list of items that need special care when being packed, such as your antique lamp or china cup-and-saucer collection.

▲ Discard flammable materials. Empty gas tanks on mowers and chain saw.

▲ Be sure to leave space open in your driveway or on the street for your truck, trailer, or moving van.

▲ Keep handy a small box of tools to dismantle furniture, plus a bucket, rags, and cleaning products to clean your home after it is empty.

Loading Your Van, Truck, or Trailer

▲ Park next to the widest door of your home and leave enough room to extend a ramp if necessary.

▲ Load your vehicle one quarter at a time, using all the space from floor to ceiling. Try to load weight evenly from side to side to prevent it from shifting.

▲ Put the heaviest items in front.

▲ Tie off each quarter with rope. This will keep your goods from banging against each other and getting damaged.

▲ Use a dolly or hand truck for heavy items. (These can be rented from rental equipment or moving companies.) CAUTION: When lifting heavy objects, bend your knees and use your leg muscles. Keep your back as straight as possible.

▲ Fit bicycles and other odd-shaped items along the walls of the truck or on top of stacked items.

Finish cleaning up your house, lock your door, and you're on your way!

$ Save Money When Buying Your Next Car $

Buying a car is the third-biggest expense you will have, after your home and taxes. You can lose and waste more money over the years in buying cars than in any other purchase. There are few good deals when buying a car, yet owning a car can be a personal pleasure instead of a financial drain.

A car should never be considered an investment (except possibly an antique or vintage model). Normally a car starts to lose money as soon as you drive it off the lot. An automobile is an expense, which means it is a financial loss. What you want to do is minimize this loss.

Over the whole period of your life you could buy or lease 20 different cars at a cost of $250,000, plus an additional $150,000 on interest, unnecessary options, and gimmick features. Any savings off this $400,000 can mean a sizable benefit for you! Here are several strategies you can use to save a lot of money.

Have a plan and don't weaken. Determine one or several models of cars you would like to own. Window-shop (don't get sucked in by a good salesman) the new-car lots to get a better idea of what you want. The best buy is normally found in a two-year-old car.

Hunt the classifieds for your ideal car. Shop the automobile classified section of your newspaper or your local *Auto Trader* magazine. (Since these ads are charged by the number of lines printed, you will need to decode the ads. If you have a problem, just call and ask the seller what equipment is listed.)

Buy your next car from an individual instead of a dealer. A private-party seller is usually the most motivated of all sellers. After several days of advertising, phones ringing, and people making ridiculous offers, the seller is happy to talk to a real person. You are in the driver's seat because there are hundreds of cars for sale by individuals and you are one buyer. People usually don't advertise a car for sale unless they believe they really need to sell it. You usually have a motivated seller who is waiting for a reasonable offer.

Buy the car you want, but only after it is 2 to 2½ years old. In fact, by using this strategy you will not only save money but get a better car than if you buy new.

When you buy a brand-new car, it depreciates about 20 percent as soon as you drive it off the lot. Yes, for a $15,000 car you automatically lose $3000. In the first two years your new car will depreciate approximately 40 percent. Let someone else lose this 40 percent, but not you. You also miss all the nonsense charges of extra freight, rustproofing, fabric coating, added warranties, etc.

One of the reasons often given for wanting to buy a new car instead of a used car is that with a used car you are buying someone else's troubles. That used to be, but not as much anymore. In the first two years the owner has had his car back and forth to the dealership working out all the bugs. If in doubt, pay a mechanic you trust to do an inspection before you purchase. You will be amazed at the savings.

Don't finance your car at the dealership. We live in a world of convenience, and it is certainly convenient to get everything done at the time of purchase, but when you do you will be paying extra interest for your loan. The dealer is really just a middleman for the finance company. You as a consumer can go directly to your bank or credit union and get a much better deal. Go to your bank or credit union and get preapproved for a loan before you go out to buy that car.

Stay out of the finance office of the dealership. That's where you weaken, because you have already agreed on a price and the monthly payments, but a sharp manager can add another $25 per month without you getting too excited. "What's $25 a month? I can certainly afford that." A quick calculation is that $25 a month over 60 months is an additional cost to you of $1500 over the life of the loan.

Never use a dealer's Blue Book. Many buyers get a copy of a Blue Book and think they have all the information they need to really lock in on a price. Or they ask the salesperson to bring out his copy (which is usually marked up higher than your copy) and you negoti ate from that. A better guide is the "National Automobile Dealers Association (NADA) Official Used Car Guide." You can get copies of this easily.

In buying a car, you can lose on two ends of your purchase:

Front-end loading is what is added to the price of the car by the salesperson. This includes:

▲ Inflated delivery and setup charges

▲ Overpriced options

▲ Phony discount or trade-in price

▲ Rustproofing, fabric protection, and paint sealant

Back-end loading is what is added in the finance department. This includes:

▲ Credit life insurance

▲ Credit disability insurance

▲ Inflated interest charges

▲ Extended warranty

That's why you must have a plan and not get sold things you don't need.

Use the NADA Official Used Car Guide to determine the value of your car. You can buy this guide at many bookstores for under $15. It is published in nine geographic regions. Call this number to get a subscription: 800-544-6232 (800-523-3110 in Virginia). It is most important for you to know exactly what any car you are looking at is actually worth, which is the maximum you will pay for that car. Never buy or sell a car without consulting the NADA Guide, and never pay more than the auction price. The average trade-in is the auction price and represents what a dealer could buy or sell the car for at an auction.

With a little practice you will be able to decode this guide book.

Fabric coat your seat covers yourself and forget the paint sealer. Fabric coating consists of about $10 worth of Scotchguard, which you could apply yourself. You don't have to pay a dealer several hundred dollars to do the same thing. It will only take you 15 minutes to do the same job yourself. Be sure to read the directions on the back of the can.

Your paint will do fine without the paint sealant with just normal maintenance of washing and waxing your car on a regular basis. If your paint does begin to fade, purchase a can of "fine grit rubbing compound" available at an auto parts store. It will bring back the shine. Remember to read the instructions on the back of the container.

Avoid undercoating your car. You don't need this added expense; the undercarriage of the car is already painted with rustproofing material by the manufacturer.

Don't pay inflated delivery and dealer preparation charges. A dealer can charge whatever he wants for delivery. His sticker price is usually higher than the actual price, since dealers get excellent rates with their railroad and trucking firms. Negotiate this price.

Dealer "setup and preparation charges" should be zero. The only costs are usually a vacuum job and a good washing. There are no other industries which charge you for delivering a product. You need not pay one when you purchase a car.

Don't fall for low interest rates or rebates. When manufacturers and dealers have extra inventory they need to have a way to sell their backlog of cars. One way is to offer you a lower interest rate or a rebate, which is really a "buy-down." The housing industry has used this for some time. You initially think this is a good deal, but it really isn't. Without going into a lengthy explanation of how it works, the bottom line is to negotiate your own deal and do your own financing.

Never finance your car for more than 36 months. Anything over this amount of time means you have a negative balance due on your car (more than it is worth). This means that in two years, if you decide to sell your car, you will find out you owe more than it's worth. The longer the term of your loan, the greater the percentage of each payment that goes to pay interest rather than principal on your loan.

A 36-month loan allows you to pay off your loan faster than your car is depreciating. This way you can sell your car anytime you want to without losing money. You don't owe more than you own.

$ Sell Your Car Yourself and Save $

"Utterly worthless!" says the buyer as he haggles over the price. But afterwards he brags about his bargain.

—Proverbs 20:14 TLB

The easy way to sell your car is to trade it in with the purchase of your next car, but when you do that you are throwing away at least $1000. I know—out of sight, out of mind. But how long do you have to work to clear $1000 after taxes? For most of us, it's a lot of hours of labor. I think it's worth the time and effort to sell your own used car. Here are some hints to help you.

Use the NADA Guide to determine your car's true value. Determine the average trade-in price, which is the minimum you will take for your car. If your car is exceptionally clean, you can usually sell it for between the trade-in and the retail price. The potential buyer will save hundreds of dollars by purchasing your car.

Meet with your banker. You will get a lot more telephone calls if you can put in your ad "Financing arranged." Meet with your present loan officer on your car and tell him or her of your intent to sell your car. Ask what would be required for someone to take over the loan. You will be told that there would need to be a new application made for the loan, and the prospect would have to have good credit. If the prospect is approved, the bank would be glad to make the new loan.

Clean your car with a good detailing job. A $50 investment in a good detailing job is well worth the investment. It will make your car look and smell new. We recommend that you have your car detailed at least once a year (and if possible twice a year), to keep your car finish well-maintained. In addition to detailing, you will want to:

▲ Have the engine steam-cleaned.

▲ Remove corrosion from the battery cables.

▲ Have all rattles tightened.

▲ Buy new floor mats for the front floor.

▲ Touch up any chipped paint.

▲ Make sure your car runs well.

Advertise your car. Run an ad in your local paper. See if there is a special for three or four days. Here are key words which stand out for buyers: low mileage, clean, sharp, like new, must sell, financing available. Include your phone number and when you can be called. Limit the times people can call by saying, "Call 5-7 P.M. weekdays, 10 A.M.-5 P.M. weekends." Put your asking price in the ad. Make your asking price $200 to $400 above the trade-in value in the NADA Guide.

Minimize the time people can see your car. To save yourself a lot of time and hassle, set up one or two specific times for people to see your car. If they call, say, "I'll be home from 5 to 6 P.M. on Saturdays to show the car." This way several people will arrive during a short period of time to give the impression that a lot of people are interested in your car. This also saves you a lot of your valuable time.

Never give your keys to a potential buyer. Always ride with the buyer; there are many scam artists who would like to take your car for a test drive and never return! The potential driver should be perfectly free to drive your car, but not alone. If there is a man of the house, he should be the one going with the potential driver. A woman should not go with a stranger.

Be excited about your car. Don't oversell, but be enthusiastic about the car you are selling. Give a reasonable, positive reason for selling it. If the buyer comments negatively about a feature of the car, you might comment, "That's why the price is so reasonable." Be positive.

Select a bottom price. Your ad should indicate a price of $200 to $400 above the rock-bottom price you will take. Once the buyer has negotiated to that price, let him know that you will not sell the car below that price. At that point the buyer will either purchase the car or excuse himself.

Have your paperwork ready. You will need to have all the necessary papers available and ready to give the new buyer, particularly if he or she needs to go to the bank for financing. However, if he doesn't have a bank for a loan, he may need to go with you to your bank to make necessary application for a loan. In some cases a buyer will pay in cash.

Accept only cash or a certified check. Never accept a personal check or a promise. Take the car off the market only when you have a reasonable deposit. If the buyer has only a check, accompany the buyer to his or her bank to cash the check.

If the buyer has financed the purchase of your car, require him to have the necessary insurance, license, and proof of ownership before taking the car. If you have been paid cash on the spot and the necessary transfer papers have been signed (they may be obtained at the bank or the local Department of Motor Vehicles), the buyer may take possession. Remove your license plate before the car leaves your home (unless the plates are to be transferred.)

Follow your state's transfer regulations. Contact your state's Department of Motor Vehicles to find out exactly what must be done legally to transfer the car from you to the new owner. Do not let the buyer take the car if your name is still listed as owner; an accident might make you liable for damages. After making a legal transfer, prepare and sign a bill of sale (a stationery store will usually carry these, or you may get them at the DMV). Keep a copy for your records, and the new owner receives a copy.

Don't cancel your insurance too fast. Wait until your loan shows "paid in full" by your lender. Also, be sure to remember to eventually cancel your insurance. If not, you will be paying for services which you aren't using.

Have the Wedding You Want While Keeping Costs Down

A man shall leave his father and his mother, and shall cleave to his wife, and they shall become one flesh.

—Genesis 2:24

When Emilie and I were married, we certainly didn't have to worry about high costs, because neither side had much money. We knew we were going to have a very modest wedding. There were no videos, limousines, carriages, garden receptions with live birds, or large entourages of attendants.

Times have changed, though, and today almost everyone wants an elaborate wedding and reception. We know of parents who have had to take out loans to pay for that wonderful occasion. According to *Brides Magazine*, the average wedding costs $16,000!

You can have a wonderful wedding and still pay only a moderate price. Wedding bells don't have to mean wedding bills. We look at a wedding as the *event* of a lifetime, not as the *debt* of a lifetime. In order to control the cost of this most sacred occasion, you must have proper planning and a budget. Here are some ways to cut corners on spiraling costs.

Planning

▲ Establish a budget and stick to it.

▲ The longer the engagement, the more money the wedding will cost.

▲ When hiring any service, discuss in detail what is included. Don't be afraid to ask questions. Question each item and delete those items you don't want. Leave nothing to oral agreement. Be sure everything is spelled out in a contract that you read before signing. Have the vendor sign and then request a copy of the contract for your file. Make sure you read each contract so you know whether your photographer can send an assistant to take your wedding pictures, or whether flank steak can be substituted for the prime rib you ordered.

▲ The cost can be eased if you purchase smaller items gradually, such as the cake knife set, toasting glasses, ringbearer's pillow, guest book, wedding favors, etc. Purchase a little here and a little there.

▲ Decide early how the wedding reception and honeymoon are going to be paid. Historically most of the costs are borne by the bride's family, with minor costs paid for by the groom's parents. Depending on the financial situation of each, you may want to make other arrangements. Just make sure there is a clear understanding of who pays for what. If this isn't clear, there can be embarrassment and hard feelings. You don't need either on such a festive occasion.

▲ Make sure you reserve the church, pastor, reception location, photographer, and caterers early, because wedding services are subject to the laws of supply and demand. If your wedding is planned for the last Saturday in June, demand is high. Consequently you have limited bargaining power, plus arrangements and facilities fill up early.

Wedding Consultants

▲ Many churches have wedding coordinators who can be of great assistance to you. They are familiar with the staff and facilities and have previous contacts with florists, musicians, and caterers.

▲ A friend or relative might be available to help coordinate these details for you. Make sure he or she has the proper temperament for getting things done.

▲ You may even want to hire a professional wedding consultant to help plan and coordinate this event. Consultants cost additional money, but they can usually save you more than they cost. Just make sure you have in writing what their service covers.

One-Stop Planners

▲ In many areas you can use the services of a one-stop consultant, usually associated with a chapel or garden, who will coordinate, sell bride's and bridesmaid's gowns, rent tuxedos, print announcements, and provide catering, flowers, photographs, wedding cake, music, and limousines or a horse and buggy. Look in your local phone directory for such services.

Clothing

▲ Tell salespersons your price ceiling. This is an area that can cause a lot of stress. You must be firm with yourself to stay in budget.

▲ Shop early for better selections. Negotiate prices if you've found the same dress for less elsewhere.

▲ Shop out of season. Hit clearance racks in late summer or early fall for next year's weddings.

▲ Purchase discontinued styles for reduced prices.

▲ Ask if the manufacturer will downgrade fabric; substitute polyester chanting for silk chanting or omit handworked beading.

▲ Get alterations quoted in writing before buying. Avoid major alterations (such as changing a neckline or waistline); these can be costly. Although most dresses need at least some minor alteration, you can limit the cost by taking careful measurements and then asking to see the manufacturer's size chart. Sizes do vary between dressmakers, and they are not likely to be the same as sizes in street clothes.

▲ Ask about the deposit. The store does need money in advance to ensure you'll really buy the dress when it comes in. But make sure you use a credit card. Why? More than one bridal shop has gone out of business, taking customers' deposits with them. If you buy with a credit card, federal consumer protection laws allow individuals to notify the card issuer and get the deposit back. If you pay by check, your chances of getting the money back are far slimmer.

▲ You might consider consignment and rental shops.

▲ Choose a fabric shoe that can be dyed after the wedding for everyday use.

▲ Some rental shops will provide the groom's tuxedo for free when you rent the ushers' tuxedos.

Time and Place

▲ Book locations in off-peak months (November through April) for possible reduced rates. Hotel deals also may be offered for weekday or weeknight weddings.

▲ You may be able to negotiate a better price if you book more than a year ahead.

▲ Check out rural sites, large garden yards, and college and boarding schools with gracious halls and libraries. Contact your state tourism board and Chamber of Commerce for addresses of mansions, country inns, or town halls. Look into parks and publicly owned buildings that may require a minimal contribution in lieu of a rental fee.

▲ Price a home wedding. You will eliminate the site fee. However, rentals of tableware and tents can be steep. You will also need to supply food and cleanup.

▲ Be careful what hour you wed. Be aware that lunch is almost always less expensive than dinner, even when the menu is the same.

Reception

▲ Limit the number of guests—that's the number one rule for savings.

▲ Plan your menu carefully. Chicken costs less than beef or veal. Broccoli costs less than asparagus.

▲ Serve food that is in season and vegetables that are grown locally.

▲ Go ethnic. Mediterranean, Mexican, German, or Chinese are often less expensive than meat and potatoes.

▲ Control your beverage offerings.

▲ The least expensive option is to have the reception between the hours of 2 P.M. and 5 P.M., when no meals are expected. An evening wedding can be followed with a "dessert reception," where guests are offered a wide array of pastries and cakes.

▲ Limit an evening reception to three or four hours to reduce beverage and labor costs. Serve hot and cold hors d'oeuvres.

▲ Consider a pre-dinner reception from noon to 4 P.M. or from 2 P.M. to 6 P.M. You might have an English high tea; hors d'oeuvres and cake; casual, open-air reception with fruits, vegetables, and cheeses; or a buffet of sliced meat, meat pies, breads, condiments, and various salads.

Guest Accommodations

▲ Negotiate a group discount if you reserve a block of rooms for out-of-town guests at a hotel. If yours is a hotel reception, check for additional discounts on room rates that the hotel may offer to your guests.

Music

▲ Consider hiring the musicians affiliated with your church or synagogue.

▲ Interview student musicians from your local college or music academy.

▲ Use a disc jockey with a good selection of records.

▲ Consider three or four musicians instead of a six-piece band.

▲ Hire a harpist, pianist, or organist for an intimate wedding.

▲ Have musicians among family or friends be part of the wedding ceremony.

Flowers

▲ Consult a florist at least three months before the wedding. In-season flowers are usually the best buy.

▲ Choose multiple blooms of inexpensive flowers, such as baby's breath and carnations worked into ferns.

▲ Use a cascade of just one type of flower and greenery. These cost less for the florist to make.

▲ Let your flowers do double duty as decorations for both the ceremony and reception.

▲ Potted plants and balloons make good attractive centerpieces.

▲ You need not decorate every row of pews or every table with flowers. Some people decorate the first few rows or every other table.

Photography

▲ Shop around, compare prices, sign a contract. Word of mouth is a good way to be satisfied.

▲ Discuss options carefully. Packages may turn out to be more expensive due to hidden costs. Negotiate prices. Arrange to take group shots before the ceremony, rather than have the photographer come to your home for family portraits, or to shoot between wedding and reception. If you want a formal portrait, ask the photographer to bring a backdrop to the reception and shoot there, saving time and money.

▲ Choose fewer prints for your album. Ask how long the photographer will keep the negatives. You may be better off to buy additional pictures in the future.

▲ Create your own albums from guests' candids.

▲ If you want a video made of your wedding, go through the same procedure as with your photographer.

Transportation

▲ Consider using sedan-sized cars of close friends and relatives for transporting your wedding party. Limousines are hired by the hour, usually with a three-to-four-hour minimum.

Honeymoon

▲ Consider a travel agency that has a wedding registry so guests can make a gift donation toward your trip. Make arrangements as soon as you set the date.

▲ Check prepackaged tours for good value, which may include air travel, hotel, food, and sightseeing.

▲ Travel off-season to get lower rates.

▲ For greater savings, book airfare, rental car, and hotel at one time. If airfares go down, be sure to have your tickets rewritten for the lesser rate.

▲ Check to see if any of your organizational memberships offer you lower rates.

▲ Use your frequent-flier miles.

▲ Let hotels know that you are on your honeymoon. Many times they have extra features with a honeymoon package.

Do It Yourself

▲ Cooperate with your friends and family to help reduce wedding costs. Get married at a friend's home, and have friends videotape the wedding. Family members can provide first or last courses to the meal. Turn your rehearsal dinner and reception into an old-fashioned potluck supper. Have a homemade cake.

▲ Fresh fruit and flowers make simple toppers. Garden flowers can be tied with ribbon and lace into bouquets. Create dried rose-petal potpourri as favors.

▲ Use artistic and musical talents of friends.

▲ Make tapes of your favorite songs as a friend stands in as D.J. Relatives can even chauffeur the wedding party.

NOTES

Chapter 1: Schedule a Plan, Plan a Schedule
1. Charles J. Givens, *Financial Self-Defense* (New York: Simon and Schuster, 1990), p. 17.
2. Ibid., p. 17.

Chapter 2: Why You Do What You Do
1. Adapted from Givens, *Financial Self-Defense*, pp. 23-24.

Chapter 3: Goals: A Dream with a Deadline
1. Emilie Barnes, *Survival for Busy Women* (Eugene, OR: Harvest House Publishers, 1986), pp. 16, 43.

Chapter 4: Writing Your Financial Goals
1. Adapted from Givens, *Financial Self-Defense*, pp. 28-57.

Chapter 9: Four Cornerstones for Money Management
1. Patrick M. Morley, *The Man in the Mirror* (Brentwood, TN: Wolgemuth & Hyatt, 1989), pp. 144-45.

Chapter 10: Four Little-Known Secrets
1. Ibid., pp. 142-43.

Chapter 12: Principles for Financial Responsibility
1. We are indebted to Charles O. White, a local Christian attorney and tax practitioner, for sharing his insight on the topics of giving, receiving, and spending. Mr. White has conducted "Personal and Family Financial Success" seminars for more than 15 years

Chapter 15: Suggested Categories for Your System
1. From Givens, *Financial Self-Defense*, pp. 41-42.

Chapter 30: Seven Ways to Get Greater Returns
1. Summarized from Peter A. Dickinson, *Retirement Wealth-Building Guide* (Potomac, MD: Phillips Publishing, 1992), p. 17.

Chapter 32: Principles of Long-Term Investing
1. Many of the ideas in this chapter were condensed and summarized from Shearson, Lehman and Hutton's booklet "The Real Definition of Investing," #GP2043.

Chapter 34: Compound Interest: The Eighth Wonder of the World
1. These principles adapted from Merrill J. Oster, *Becoming a Man of Honor* (San Bernardino, CA: Here's Life Publishers, 1988), pp. 69-70.

Chapter 47: How to Cut Your Family's Medical Bills
1. Many of these ideas are adapted from Peter A. Dickinson, *The Retirement Letter* (Potomac, MD: Phillips Publishing, Inc., May 1992), pp. 1-4.

Chapter 48: Ways to Stretch Your Dollars
1. Many of these ideas are adapted from Dickinson, *Retirement Wealth-Building Guide*, pp. 22-24.

For more information regarding speaking engagements and additional material, please send a self-addressed stamped envelope to:

More Hours In My Day
2838 Rumsey Drive
Riverside, CA 92506
(909) 682-4714